THE ESSENTIAL

North Carolina Driver's License Handbook

ELS SERIES

KNOWLEDGE, IN EVERY LANE

ISBN: 9798392123391

CBMA02022416

THE ESSENTIAL NORTH CAROLINA DRIVER'S LICENSE HANDBOOK

Foreword

The journey to becoming a licensed driver can be both exciting and nerve-wracking. What's more, the importance of being a licensed driver is immense.

For this reason, we've created the Essential a state-specific collection of handbooks designed to help you confidently pass your driver's license knowledge test and embark on a lifetime of safe and responsible driving.

Our main objective is to prepare you thoroughly for the exam so that you don't face any difficulties during the test by making your preparation accurate and a fun experience.

QUESTIONS AS SEEN ON THE TEST:

Our dedicated team of experts has carefully curated a collection of practice questions that closely resemble those you'll encounter on test day.

Drawing on the structure of past questions, we've designed our questions to reflect real-world scenarios, helping you build the confidence and knowledge needed to tackle any challenge the test may throw your way.

CONCISE LESSONS:

This book offers concise, high-quality lessons on traffic laws, road signs, and safe driving practices.

Our engaging storytelling approach makes complex road rules and signals easy to understand, allowing you to quickly grasp the essential information you need to pass your knowledge test and become a skilled and responsible driver.

EXPLAINED ANSWERS:

To help you build a solid foundation of driving knowledge, each practice question in our material explains the correct answer.

fully grasping the reasoning behind each answer will help you better comprehend the subject at hand—improving your ability to tackle more complex topics in the future.

YOUR STATE, YOUR RULES:

Each book in the Essential is written to cater to each state's unique rules and regulations.

Moreover, learning should be relevant and engaging, which is why our handbooks focus on the information that matters most to you.

THANK YOU FOR TRUSTING ELS SERIES

Dear Future Drivers, thank you for choosing ELS SERIES.

We are truly grateful that you've chosen The Essential as your trusted guide to becoming a skilled driver. In a world filled with countless options, we're honored that you've trusted our study aid book to support your quest to become a licensed driver. Your determination to become an exceptional driver is inspiring, and we're thrilled to be a part of it.

The Essential team has dedicated their hearts, expertise, and passion to crafting this book series with one goal and one goal only: helping you get your driver's license in the best (and easiest!) way possible. We understand the learning challenges you're facing and are committed to serving as steadfast companions you can lean on every step of the way.

Your trust in us means the world, and we truly value you as our customer. A heartfelt thank you to each one of you!

THE ELS SERIES TEAM

FOR MORE AMAZING
PRODUCTS, VISIT OUR
AMAZON AUTHOR PAGE BY
SCANNING THIS QR CODE

SCAN ME

ELS SERIES

THE ESSENTIAL NORTH CAROLINA DRIVER'S HANDBOOK

Contents   Page

THE ESSENTIAL NORTH CAROLINA DRIVER'S HANDBOOK

Content   Page

The North Carolina Division of motor vehicles (NCDMV) is tasked with developing driver competency to improve safety on the roads. The NCDMV also seeks to maintain all valid driver's licenses (so long as it is safe for them to do so) and acknowledges that the freedom/mobility afforded **by this privilege** is vital for most residents' quality of life: speaking to the importance of **an adequate testing** system to **determine one's ability** to operate a specific type of vehicle.

Getting your driver's license in North Carolina can take different paths. Adults or new residents (+18 years old) in this state can directly opt for a class C driver's license. On the other hand, minors follow a multi-stage process called the **Graduated Driver's License Program** for teenagers who are at **least 15 years** old and have a **Driving Eligibility Certificate** granted from their school.

Eventually, this program is **composed of three levels.** You start with a **limited license** (Level One), then progress to **the limited Provisional License** (Level Two), and finally, **the full Provisional License** (Level Three), culminating in a full Class C license. This program is specifically designed to give new motorists a chance to gradually improve their driving skills and extend their practice of driving over time.

LICENSE CLASSIFICATION

Understanding how driver's licenses work involves realizing they're designed for specific types of vehicles. In North Carolina, for instance, if you're planning to drive regular cars, pickups, or vans, **you'd be getting a class C license.**

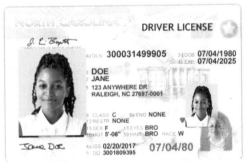

North Carolina driver's license as depicted in the image, is a durable plastic card featuring a combination of white, light red, yellow, and blue colors. This card showcases essential details such as your name, photograph, and other identifying information. Additionally, it includes an expiration date, necessitating timely renewal before it lapses.

Digital imaging is employed to capture and store customer photos and signatures. Renewals for driver's licenses are permitted **up to six months** before the customer's birthday.

It is advised for customers to initiate the renewal process early to guarantee the timely arrival of their new license.

Upon the request of a police officer, individuals operating a motor vehicle must present **their valid driver's license, along with insurance and registration documents.**

In case of **an address change or a name change** from the details on your driver's license, please inform the division **within 60 days** and obtain a duplicate license reflecting the updated information.

ELIGIBILITY FOR A NORTH CAROLINA DRIVER'S LICENSE

New residents are given a 60-day window to obtain a North Carolina license or learner permit after establishing residence. Not only that! If applying for a Class C License, there may be a need to undergo tests like knowledge, and vision tests. and, if deemed necessary by the examiner, a driving skills test.

As a newcomer to North Carolina, aged 15 to 18, and holding a learner permit, it's advisable to reach out to your local driver's license office. They can help determine the type of license or learner permit you are eligible for.

To add, you are considered a resident of this state if you have employment in North Carolina, pay for college/university tuition, own property, or register to vote in local/state elections.

THE EXAMINATION PROCEDURE

If you wish to get your driver's license in the state of North Carolina you must follow this testing process :

1. **Meeting the vision standards**

2. **Passing the Knowledge test (Road sign recognition and Rules of the road)**

3. **Passing the Driving skills test**

VISION REQUIREMENTS

You need to demonstrate the ability to meet the vision requirements when you apply for your first issued driver's license

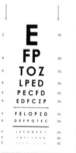

A representative will ask you to read lines of letters with both eyes open at first, then with each eye separately. Each phase of the exam will be guided by the employee.

If a driver wears glasses or contact lenses, their license will have a restriction requiring them to wear them while operating a vehicle. Drivers who wear telescopic lenses must meet certain criteria and undergo extra vision testing to obtain a license.

The vision test does not require the removal of contact lenses. Your driver's license, on the other hand, will be confined to **"vision correction."**

THE KNOWLEDGE TEST

One of the main goals of assignments in the driver's license knowledge test is to assess the candidate's knowledge and mastery of topics related to **rules of the road and safe driving practices, state-specific regulations, and the ability to comprehend traffic signs and signals and act accordingly**.

Class C knowledge exams are also accessible in a variety of languages. Candidates are still required to demonstrate their ability to understand road signs in English.

The North Carolina driver's license knowledge examination includes:

* **25 multiple-choice** questions

* you must properly answer at least **20 of them** to pass.

* You can make an appointment via the NCDMV official website.

* The questions have **4 options** to choose from and one of them is the correct answer.

To successfully pass the traffic signs section, you need to recognize traffic signs based on their color and shape, providing an explanation for the meaning of each.

Individuals who do not successfully pass the knowledge or driving test for a standard Class C license have the option to retake the test after a waiting period of seven days.

DRIVING SKILLS TEST

To demonstrate that you can safely operate a motor vehicle by adhering to the rules of the road, you will be evaluated on your driving skills in an on-the-road test. It is a mandatory step after passing all other tests.

To add, The driving test is obligatory when applying for a license for the first time and may also be necessary for license renewal. Nevertheless, it is not a requirement for a learner permit.

Your behind-the-wheel test car must be safe to drive, have a valid registration, and be fully insured. Other passengers are generally not authorized during this examination. **You are required to wear your safety belt!**

PROVISIONAL LICENSING

Administrable requirements to be eligible for the learner program in North Carolina

You can apply for your first issued permit in North Carolina as soon as you are 15 years old but not older than 18 years old, however, you should meet the requirements that consist of presenting a **Driving Eligibility Certificate**, or if you've graduated from high school, just show the DMV a proof such as your diploma.

There's more to this! You've got to have the receipts for completing a driver education course, think 30 hours of in-the-classroom education program and 6 hours behind the wheel, getting the real feel of the road.

THE PHASE 1: LIMITED LEARNER PERMIT (1 YEAR)

Successful completion of knowledge and vision tests is a prerequisite.

All passengers must use seat belts or child safety seats. While The front seat is restricted to only the driver and the supervising driver.

During the first six months with a level one permit, driving is allowed between 5 a.m. and 9 p.m., accompanied by a supervising driver. After six months from level one issuance, driving is permitted at any time, still with a supervising driver.

A Driving Log must be maintained, documenting at least 60 hours of operation. Daytime driving extends from sunrise to sunset, while nighttime driving occurs after sunset and before daylight.

THE PHASE 2: LIMITED PROVISIONAL LICENSE (6 MONTHS)

Driving without supervision is permitted between 5 a.m. and 9 p.m. and at any time when commuting directly to or from work or any volunteer fire, rescue, or emergency medical service if you are a member.

All passengers must use seat belts or child safety seats. While the supervising driver must be seated beside the driver.

A Driving Log must be completed, detailing a minimum of 12 hours of operation, with at least six hours during nighttime. Daytime driving extends from sunrise to sunset, while nighttime driving occurs after sunset and before daylight.

THE PHASE3: FULL PROVISIONAL LICENSE

During this phase, restrictions placed on your licence from phases 1 and 2, such as nighttime driving limitations, seatbelt obligation, mandatory supervision requirements and the use of driving log **do not apply.**

TRAFFIC SIGNAL RULES

Traffic at intersections may be controlled by utilizing **_traffic signals_** that employ green, yellow, and red lights. Whichever lane of traffic has **the right-of-way** is determined by the color of the light. A horizontal or a vertical traffic signal may be used.

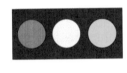

RED LIGHT

In the event of **_solid red light,_** drivers are required to come to a **full stop** (before the stop line or crosswalk). This rule applies at any intersection even where there is no crosswalk or stop line. To avoid accidents, drivers must wait for the green light before proceeding through the intersection.

PROCEEDING AT A RED LIGHT

The first thing you need to know is if **turning right at a red light** is allowed in the location where you drive.

In the state of North Carolina, right turns on red **are allowed** if they can be accomplished safely unless a **road sign** indicates otherwise.

After a full stop, yield to other traffic and pedestrians on both your lane and the right lane crosswalk.

The only left turn authorized at a **red light** is into a **one-way street from a one-way street** unless a sign prohibits the turn. To make this turn, drivers must bring their vehicles to a full stop, and only then may they proceed.

FLASHING RED LIGHT

When facing a **flashing red light** put your vehicle to a complete stop, look for traffic from all sides of the intersection ahead, and if clear you can then proceed.

The easiest way to deal with flashing red lights is **to treat them as stop signs**, Always come to a full stop, check the intersection and yield the right of way to others who got to the intersection before you, and then proceed when the way is clear.

GREEN ARROW WITH RED LIGHT

When confronted with a traffic signal that has both a green arrow and a red control light, drivers may pass through the intersection **only in the direction indicated by the arrow** without stopping.

YELLOW LIGHT

Yellow lights mean that you need to come to a full stop. Unless you are closer than one vehicle length to the intersection, than you are going to proceed through. do it defensively by covering the brakes, making sure you are scanning the intersection and that there aren't any road users. If you are farther back from the intersection than one vehicle length you need to come to a full stop.

FLASHING YELLOW LIGHT

flashing yellow light need to be treat it similarly **to a yield sign.** Continue cautiously after allowing pedestrians to cross and other vehicles to pass. You should slow down but not stop if there is no traffic on your way.

GREEN LIGHT

If the traffic control light is solid green, drivers may go through the intersection without stopping or slowing down if they drive within the speed limit, unless they must yield to **oncoming vehicles** when **turning left** or to **pedestrians in the crosswalk** when turning right or left.

When turning left, start off by getting into the leftmost of the lane to get ready to take the left-hand turn,

as you get closer to the intersection check that there is no oncoming traffic that you may obstruct and then also make sure that there are no pedestrians crossing or about to cross. While arriving at the intersection, check your rear-view mirror as well as your left side mirror and blind spots. You can then proceed to make the left turn in the correct manner.

FLASHING GREEN LIGHT

A flashing green light is **rarely used** and can mean two things, either you can move forward freely as traffic at the intersection will be free because **all directions are stopped by a red light,** and therefore, there is less risk for obstruction. Or it can mean that the signal can be **pedestrian-activated**, thus use extra caution.

GREEN ARROW WITH GREEN LIGHT

There is no need for drivers to **yield** to the direction indicated by the arrow when they see a traffic control light with a **green arrow and a solid green** traffic control light. When it is safe and lawful, drivers who are facing the green light may likewise travel in the other direction.

Remember: If you are approaching an intersection and the traffic lights are **not working**, you should treat it as **a 4-way stop sign** intersection and apply the suitable right-of-way rules *(See Page 34).*

There are some different types of yield signs that you may observe as per your state rules, some would even ask you to **yield on solid green or yellow lights**. Be cautious when you encounter these signs on the road.

PEDESTRIAN SIGNALS AND SIGNS

Pedestrian safety is a priority for the state of North Carolina. In order to anticipate the activities of others with whom you share the road, drivers must be familiar with pedestrian control signals. When it is safe to do so, pedestrians facing a traffic light with the word **"WALK"** or a similar symbol may cross the road. As long as the word or symbol appears, pedestrians may continue to cross and clear the intersection. **Countdown timers** may be seen on certain pedestrian signals to let pedestrians know how much time is left before the light changes.

If the text or symbol **"DON'T WALK"** appears on a traffic light, then a pedestrian must not cross the intersection.

 "WALK" is signalled by this pedestrian signal.

 "DON'T WALK" or **"WAIT"** signs for pedestrians

 When the flashing **"DON'T WALK"** or the flashing upraised hand begins:

A. If you are already in the street, proceed to finish crossing.

B. If you have not yet left the curb, refrain from starting to cross.

School zones or areas, playground zones or areas, school crossings, and pedestrian crossings all have yellow lights on a sign with a symbol to convey caution. It is mandatory for drivers to slow down to a maximum of 20 mph while the yellow lights are flashing and to yield or stop for pedestrians.

Pedestrian crossing signs with **yellow lights.**

Pedestrians must follow the regulations for the color of light they are facing at intersections with traffic control signals that lack pedestrian **WALK** and **DON'T WALK** signals.

• *Red light*; Do not cross the street at this time.

• *Yellow light*; Avoid entering the junction if you're already there.

• *Green light*; Proceed, Any designated or unmarked crosswalks may be used to cross the street.

Pedestrians should always look both ways before crossing the street.

IMPORTANT: The common signs that a pedestrian crossing the road is blind include carrying a **white cane** and being accompanied by a **guide dog**

Lane reversals are employed to manage traffic flow in specific lanes, with reversible lanes being a common application. Reversible lanes, which adjust traffic direction based on the time of day, often utilize this control. The signal(s) in one or more lanes transition from a red X to a green or yellow arrow.

SOLID RED X:

 Drivers must not enter or stay in a driving lane marked with a *solid red X.* An impending traffic signal is shown by this light. The green arrow indicates that the lane is safe to enter.

DOWNWARD POINTING GREEN ARROW

 Driving in the lane with the *downward-pointing green arrow* is authorized for drivers facing the arrow's.

YELLOW ARROW DOWN TO THE LEFT OR RIGHT

 This traffic signal simply means that this lane is **about to be closed**, therefore safely merge into the direction of the arrow and give the way to vehicles already present.

ROAD SIGNS

Road signs come in various shapes and colors, and memorizing the significance of each traffic sign can be challenging for some road users.

Nevertheless, studying them and understanding what each category is supposed to mean based on colors and shapes is a key point toward a quicker understanding of what you are being demanded to do for optimal safety.

Traffic signs convey information to road users via 3 variables

A. The color of the sign
B. The shape of the sign
C. The symbols and/or writing on the sign

COLOR CODING

 RED :
A Prohibition or a stop sign
The adoption of the red color on traffic signs is defined as a stop, a yield, or prohibition.

 YELLOW :
Warning of a danger or a caution
Some signs are colored yellow, those should be perceived as a warning.

 GREEN :
Announce traffic movement and directional instructions
The green signs are most recurrently presented on highways and freeways and they mainly show travelers the directions, the exits, or the attractions.

ORANGE :
Temporary signs often alert travelers about construction and maintenance

The orange road signs refer to temporary conditions, these signs warn travelers of unusual situations like work zones ahead, detours, lane closures, or traffic control people on the road. You should obey the instructions attentively as construction zones in most cases bring additional hazards.

WHITE :
Regulatory signs
The utilization of regulatory signs consists of the implication or reinforcement of the laws regulating traffic. Regulations that apply at all times or within a predetermined window of time or place, either on streets or highways or a general regulatory sign that governs public behavior

BLACK :
Lane control signs
The lane control signs consist of managing the flow of traffic on certain lanes by permitting or prohibiting access to them.

THE SHAPES OF ROAD SIGNS

Besides the colors, you can tell a lot about road signs by their shapes. They will give you your first piece of information. The shapes of road signs that are the most commonly found are **triangles, diamonds, rectangles, and circles.**

1/ The actions inside the circle are permitted:

2/ The actions shown inside the circle are not Allowed

3/ These shapes often reveal that a school zone or a crosswalk ahead

4/ This Sign Shows information or Instruction About Either Distance or Destination

5/ A Sign of a Regulatory Instruction Like speed limitation:

6/This sign reveal caution of a hazard ahead on the road

7/ This Sign reveals places for fuel or Food, lodging, or Assistance

8/ This Sign Inform You On a construction area or Temporary Work On the Road

9/ Reveals Lane control Ahead

REGULATORY SIGNS

The most prominent road signs are regulatory signs. The term "regulatory" is derived from the word "regulation," which refers to laws. And if it is law, it must be adhered to.

Regulatory signs unlike the other classified road signs come in various shapes. However, the commonly used colors in this specific classification are usually **red white, and black**.

Imperatively, drivers must have knowledge of these for the purposes of road tests to be successful either on the learner's or in on-road tests.

STOP SIGNS are eight-sided (octagonal shape) with a white border, and the word written on them is STOP. (Stop can be translated to Alto in Spanish) and they stand for imperative stopping at the intersection where they are placed.

YIELD SIGNS are three-sided (Downside triangle), they have large red borders and the background is white. They signal to the driver that they must give way to oncoming traffic or pedestrians when entering the road.

SPEED LIMITATIONS/ TRAFFIC MOVEMENT SIGNS are four-sided (rectangular shape) with a black border and white background. They are often speed signs but can be about

slow movement in the traffic. That is been said that drivers who drive slowly should move over to the right lane so other drivers may pass for better traffic flow.

RAILWAY CROSSING SIGNS are shaped like an X with red borders and white background. Be cautious as you drive over a train track. *(See Page 19)*

SCHOOL ZONE SIGNS are five-sided (pentagon in shape) Most of these signs are in neon green. These signs indicate that you are coming to a school area, Which implies that you need to drive with a speed limit of 20 miles per hour (*See Page 19*).

PERMISSIVE SIGNS are square in shape with black border, and the Background color is green circle, and they provide drivers with information on actions and movements they are allowed to do on the road. For example, the displayed signs mean that PARKING is allowed and the double arrow indicates that it is valid for the entire block.

PROHIBITIVE SIGNS on the other hand, are square in shape with a black border, white Background and a red circle warn drivers about actions that are not allowed on the road, for example, the displayed sign means that you are not allowed to go straight on the intersection ahead.

LANE USAGE SIGNS

They are four-sided (rectangular shape) colored white and black signs that indicate which lanes on a highway or freeway should be used for specific types of turns or movements.

These signs are typically placed above or to the side of the road and use arrows or other symbols to indicate the recommended lane usage, they are also correlated with road markings.

TRAFFIC DIRECTION LANE

Proceed in direction of the arrow only:

Two way traffic	**Two way Left turn**	**Divider ahead keep right**

Speed limit signs

The recommended maximum speed through the lane under normal conditions.

RESTRICTED USAGE LANE

In some urban centers, to improve the safety and flow of traffic, certain lanes have been reserved for specific uses, indicated by traffic signs. there are several types of restricted usage lanes that drivers should be aware of. These include:

Express Lanes: Express lanes, also known as toll lanes, are typically found on freeways. These lanes are reserved for drivers who pay a toll, or for vehicles with a certain number of passengers (carpool, vanpool). They are intended to provide a faster and more reliable trip for those willing to pay a toll.

Bus-only lanes: Bus-only lanes are designated lanes on highways and freeways that are reserved for buses only. These lanes are intended to improve the efficiency and reliability of bus service.

Bike lanes: Bike lanes are designated lanes on roads that are reserved for bicycles. They are intended to improve the safety and accessibility of biking as a mode of transportation.

Truck lanes: Some freeways have designated lanes for trucks, those lanes are intended to improve safety and mobility for truck drivers.

Also known as **"carpool lanes," high-occupancy vehicle (HOV) lanes** are designated highway/freeway lanes reserved for vehicles containing more than one passenger to ultimately encourage carpooling and reduce traffic congestion.

HOV lanes are marked with a diamond symbol and separated from regular lanes by a solid white line. The exact number of passengers required to use HOV lanes varies depending on the location and time of day (pay attention to road sign as they will display information regarding the minimum number of passengers required), in general, vehicles must have at least two or more occupants to take advantage of this benefit during rush hour.

CONSTRUCTION SIGNS

Construction signs are orange with a black stroke and the symbols or writings on them are black. Most of the time rectangular or diamond in shape. Their main role is to **warn you of potential hazards and obstructions** on the roadway, and they often indicate temporary conditions that may not be present at other times.

Construction signs are one part of a larger system that helps keep drivers safe in construction zones. Pylons, flaggers, flashing lights, signs, and even pilot vehicles may also be present to guide you through the construction zone safely. They have reduced speed limits to ensure the safety of both drivers and construction workers.

Fines for speeding in construction zones are also higher than standard speeding fines.

 This sign notifies you of the presence of flaggers at a construction site, you are **required by law** to **follow their instructions**

 This sign indicates that **there are workers** or construction sites, thus be careful and reduce your speed

Pylons on construction zones are orange and black striped, you can see in construction areas most of the time diggers that are a characteristic of construction zones. Construction zones also can be surrounded by fences, which creates a distinct physical barrier between traffic and construction zones.

GUIDE SIGNS

Guide signs communicate important information that facilitates safe navigation, including information regarding **directional guidance, intersecting roads, desirable destination distance, and the location of services on the road**. They have a green background and display their message via text or logo. Here are three instances of guide signs commonly found on highways and expressways.

SCHOOL ZONES SIGNS

The first school sign gives you an advanced notice that there is a school in and around the area and if there are children present on the roadway, reduce your speed, and don't pass vehicles traveling in the same direction.

In North Carolina, the school zone speed limit is generally **20 mph** unless a road sign says otherwise.

Pay extra caution during specified hours when children are present. generally **between 8 am and 5 pm** during school days, and to posted signs, as the speed limit may be different depending on the location. Always obey traffic laws and be aware of your surroundings when driving in a school zone .

 Passing in school zones can be incredibly dangerous. they are designated areas where children and families are crossing roads, walking to and from school, and playing. Passing in these zones increases the likelihood of accidents and children can be unpredictable.

RAILROAD CROSSING

One of the reasons why railway crossings are an important compound of the driving experience is because they present unique safety challenges, as they involve severe consequences and greater risks, due to the longer braking distance of rails and the fact that they may not necessarily keep a steady schedule.

You need to know also that **trains have always the right-of-way**. And that at night the risk of an incident multiplies as drivers don't have **a clear vision**. therefore, appropriate warning signs will be displayed to promote safety

ADVANCED WARNING SIGNS

Many railway crossings have warning signs that alert drivers beforehand that they are approaching a railway crossing. These signs are often accompanied by road markings. All railway crossings that intersect with roadways have advanced traffic control signs, signals, flashing lights, crossing gates, or even flaggers.

In the absence of signals at the railroad crossing, you should reduce your speed and be ready to stop if a train is seen or heard approaching. In the worst-case scenario, if you are stuck on a rail track and a train is on its way, leave the vehicle immediately

Under no circumstances should your vehicle come to a stop on a railroad track, and make sure to not cross a railway if there is traffic congestion or anything that will put you at risk

Note that even when the crossing gates are not down or the lights are not flashing, it is still necessary to stop, look both ways, and listen for a train before crossing the tracks.

WARNING SIGNS

The cautionary or advisory signs are the second most frequently observed signs on the roadways. Typically, they are four-sided with a diamond or rectangular shape and a yellow background. The symbols and writings on them are black.

Hazard marker objects play a crucial role in alerting drivers to potential hazards and obstructions. They indicate which side to pass on and whether passing is permitted on the right or left.

Chevron sign indicates a sharp bend in the road

CHANGING ROAD CONDITION

Hill   **Bumps**

Pavement ends   **Slippery when wet**

No passing ahead   **Falling rocks**

Hazard marker objects near the road's edge are necessary to caution drivers about potential dangers

Left   Right

Sharp turn Left   **Right turn curve**

DIVIDED HIGHWAY SIGNS

Road curves right than left   **Winding road**   **Divided highway begins**   **Divided highway ends**

Road narrows both sides

Narrow passage

Crossroad

The advisory speed limit

PAVEMENT MARKINGS

Pavement markings work in tandem with traffic signs and stoplight signals to provide crucial details regarding the traffic flow and where you may and may not go to ensure everyone's safety.

Concrete patterns (straight or broken line) Different colors and numbers (white or yellow) (single or double) play a major role in separating lanes of traffic, displaying the change in roadways, identifying pedestrian movement, highlighting obstructions, and warning when it is unsafe to overtake, change lanes or make a U-turn.

<u>Yellow line markings</u> separate traffic moving in the opposite direction, marking the center of a roadway and on divided highways, they mark the left edge. On the other hand, **White lane markings** separate traffic moving in the same direction and mark the edge of a roadway.

A Solid line marking indicates restricted movement, which means that crossing the solid line to pass or change is prohibited.

Broken line marking means that crossing the broken line to pass or change lanes is permitted.

YELLOW LANE MARKING

A **broken yellow line** mark a passing zone, you may drive on the left lane to pass other vehicles, only when it is safe to do so.

Solid yellow lines, single or double to the left of your lane indicate that passing is risky and therefore **not allowed**.

A solid yellow line along with a broken yellow line means that passing is allowed for drivers who have the broken line on their side. Nevertheless, it is prohibited for the driver with the solid yellow line on their side to pass or turn.

WHITE LANE MARKINGS

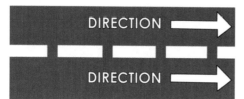

A **solid white line** in the middle of the road is used to separate traffic traveling in the same direction and indicates that crossing the line is not allowed, except in cases where it is necessary such as **avoiding an accident or a hazardous obstruction**.

It may also indicate the edge of the roadway and help drivers understand the limits of the road.

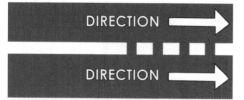

Broken or dashed white lines indicate that it is safe to cross the lines, as long as you do so when it is safe and the traffic is going in the same direction as you are.

When transitioning **from a solid to a dashed** white line, this means that you are permitted to change lanes once you have crossed over the dashed line

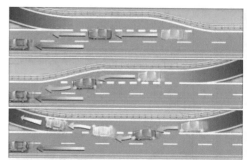

If you see **continuous lines** on your left-hand side, it usually means that the lane you are currently driving in is ending or diverging, and you will need to change lanes to continue on your intended route.

On the other hand, continuous lines on your right indicate that your lane will continue uninterrupted and you may stay in your current lane.

A **stop line** is a single white line painted across the road. It indicates that you need to stop just before the line. If there is no stop line marked, you should still stop.

You may only go in the direction indicated by the arrow.

TWO WAY LEFT TURN MARKINGS

 Solid and broken yellow lines are also used for **center left turning lanes,** which are often located on main thoroughfares in the center of the road, allowing you to turn from a major road onto a minor road.

The center lane is for left turns only - it is not a passing lane. Make sure to position your vehicle correctly in the lane so as not to block traffic.

There is also a two-way left turn center lane, which means that traffic from both directions can use the lane for left turns. You do not need to worry about collisions because if a left-turning vehicle is coming from the opposite direction, it will be a fair distance away.

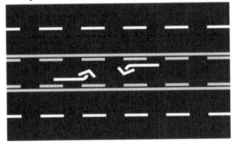

Two-way left turning center lane

RAILWAY CROSSING

 Trains always have the right-of-way. This is because trains require a significant distance to come to a stop and are less maneuverable.

Most railway crossings are marked with an X symbol and may also have electrical and mechanical warning devices such as flashing lights.

X markings indicate that you are coming to the railway crossing. If a train is approaching, you must stop and give the right of way to the train. Be sure to stop before the X marking to ensure your safety.

ACCESSIBLE PARKING VIA PERMIT ONLY

 As a holder of an accessible parking permit, it's essential that you always display your current permit on the dashboard or sun visor of the vehicle you are traveling in. This ensures that the permit number and expiry date are clearly visible to anyone who needs to see it.

The only person allowed to use the permit for parking is the individual whose name appears clearly. Using the permit for parking privileges without the permit holder present may result in severe consequences, including the suspension of the permit and a substantial penalty.

Hence, it's crucial to follow the rules related to accessible parking permits to ensure that they remain available to those who genuinely need them.

TRAFFIC ISLAND

Traffic islands are there to help traffic flow, separate lanes of traffic, and provide refuge for pedestrians.When you see yellow lines painted on an island, it means they are there to separate traffic in opposite directions. As a result, you should never drive on the island treat the yellow lines on the island as if they were solid lines, and stay on the right side of them at all times.

A Traffic island's utility relies on it's positioning on the road, generally they have a traffic control advantages in the sense that they optimize traffic flow, in other cases they may be utilized to house infrastructure such as traffic lights or signs or to channel traffic onto a desired direction or as far as a form of traffic calming by narrowing the roadway or introducing curves.

DIAMOND LANE MARKINGS

Diamonds lanes are a restricted **lanes**, that's been said, only certain vehicles meeting the posted criteria on the sign are allowed to travel on those specific **lanes**. These criteria can be either related to the type of vehicle or certain times and dates in which they can use the lane in question usually in the rush hours.

Shared used lanes or Sharrows are used to alert motorists that bicyclists may occupy the travel lane. They can also help bicyclists maintain a safe lane position.

SYMBOLS

These symbols are utilized on the pavement to aid road users. They can also be used by themselves for the purpose of alerting the driver to guide or regulate the traffic. These markings may involve:

Arrows: The movements of vehicles that are permitted in a particular lane are indicated by the arrows.

Railroad crossing road marking symbol: displayed in intersections prior to entering a railroad crossing

Facilities accessible for disabled individuals such as parking places, stairs, etc.

Diamond lanes indicate that the lane is reserved for specific types of vehicles

Sharrows This symbol marks a lane shared by motorists and bicyclists.

Your driving privilege may be suspended or revoked for a variety of reasons. One of them **is accumulating points on your driving record**. Perhaps you're already familiar with this (dreaded) point system, which is designed to penalize drivers for traffic violations and encourage safety on the road. Each traffic violation is assigned a specific number of points in this case, and drivers who accumulate too many of these within a given timeframe may face dire consequences such as a license suspension or sky-high insurance rates.

If you want to steer clear of this points system (pun intended), always obey local speed laws/limits set by the NCDMV and enforced by law enforcement: keeping an eye out for corresponding roadway signs and remembering that these limits aren't arbitrary but instead based on road/vehicle type, weather conditions, and the surrounding environs.

POINT ON YOUR RECORD

On your North Carolina driving record, you never **"lose"** your demerit points. Initially, you start with zero points. Then, when you are convicted of violating a particular traffic law, you begin to gain these points.

Reaching seven points could land you in a driver improvement clinic.

Successfully finishing the clinic knocks off **three points** from your driving record. If you amass **12 points within three years**, your license might face suspension. Moreover, gaining **eight points within three years** after a license reinstatement could lead to **a second suspension.**

Be sure to check the official NCDMV website for a comprehensive list of offenses along with their corresponding demerit points.

LAW ENFORCEMENT STOP

If a law enforcement officer instructs you to pull over, there's no need to be concerned! as it is a standard procedure and does not automatically imply that you have violated any laws.

During a Law enforcement stop by the Police make sure that the police officer acknowledges that you have noticed him **by utilizing your emergency flashers (hazard lights)**.Even if you're in a restricted usage lane, safely go to the right shoulder. And when feasible, come to a full stop.

25

- Pull over to a safe location as soon as possible. Turn on your hazard lights to indicate that you are complying.
- Unless the police tell you otherwise, stay in your vehicle.
- Sudden movements, especially reaching into pockets or the glove compartment, can be perceived as a threat. Inform the officer of your actions before making any moves.
- Make sure **your hands and the hands of all passengers are visible.** They can be on your wheel or dashboard for example.

When a car is stopped by law enforcement, the driver must present a **valid driver's license, evidence of insurance coverage, and vehicle registration.**

Motorists should always avoid interrupting or intervening with the police officer's responsibilities during the traffic stop and act as courteously as possible.

You should know also that law enforcement has **the legal authority** to search your car under certain conditions without your agreement.

YOUR DUTY AFTER A COLLISION

Unless you're directly involved or emergency aid has not yet arrived, **never stop at an auto accident** site as you can potentially block traffic or cause further hazards/potential accidents on the roadway.

It's certainly no secret that being involved in a vehicle crash resulting in bodily injury, property damage, or (tragically) death is an overwhelmingly stressful experience.

Nevertheless, you'll need to pull up your bootstraps to **provide information** and **render aid** as necessary: trying your absolute best to remain calm and follow the proper procedures, which can go a long way toward keeping everyone around safe.

You'll also need to **exchange information** for the vehicle(s), witness(es), and driver(s) involved—including **names, addresses, phone numbers, license plate numbers, and driver's license/insurance information.**

Immediately call 911 (especially if someone is hurt) or local law enforcement in the aftermath of a crash, and **turn on your hazard lights**.

Take **photos or manually sketch** the scene if necessary, showing vehicle crash locations and any other pertinent details. A law enforcement officer should complete a written report, especially (of course) if the crash involves suspicion of DUI and/or results in death, injury, or property damage.

if you experience **an accident with an unattended vehicle** (or any other type of property, for that matter), you're obligated to make every possible attempt to locate the owner and notify law enforcement about the incident. **Unable to locate** the property owner? **Leave a note** behind that includes your name, contact information, and the date/time of the accident.

According to North Carolina laws and regulations, **it is mandatory to** notify the nearest law enforcement officer or agency of any collision that results in **injury, death,** or when the combined damage to vehicles and property is estimated **at $1,000 or more.**

Failing to adhere to this reporting obligation may lead **to legal prosecution,** and there is a possibility of suspension of your driver's license. Additionally, it is advisable to report any collision to your insurance provider.

Finally, If someone is injured, apply first aid if you're trained to do so; **never attempt to move or transfer an injured person**, however, to avoid aggravating a potential neck, spinal, or other injury. If the accident involves an injured motorcyclist or bicycle rider, **avoid removing his or her helmet** for the same reason.

| FENDER BENDER |
| MOVE VEHICLES |
| FROM TRAVEL LANES |

Generally and most especially when a " **fender bender**" in other words minimal damage accident (no injuries, minor vehicle Damage sign) is displayed, all parties involved in the crash are required **to move their vehicles to the shoulder of the road** after taking pictures or drawing the position of their vehicles at the scene of the accident.

DISTRACTED DRIVING

Distracted driving is a very dangerous habit that endangers not only you and your passengers but also other vulnerable road users such as bicycles and pedestrians. Reading, writing, or sending messages on a hand-held gadget like a cell phone is prohibited by law.

Other common distractions include:

- Using a cell phone.
- Looking at something, someone, or something inside or outside the car.
- reaching for something.
- unattended pets.
- Grooming.

It is prompted not to reply to calls on your cell phone. Unless you **pull off** the road **and park** your vehicle, by then you can use your phone to answer your calls or text back.

For your best interest, familiarize yourself with all the safety and use features of any in-car electronics, including your car play or cockpit features before you start driving and it is preferable to schedule your favorite radio stations or music you often listen to well in advance.

Additionally, steer clear of engaging in complex or candid conversations with other passengers in the car

<u>Driving while fatigued might also be just as risky as distracted driving. since:</u>

- Your thinking and reaction time will be slowed down.
- Your judgment and eyesight can be affected.
- and/or you may be nodding or falling completely asleep.

DRIVING WHILE IMPAIRED

All of the critical abilities required to drive safely are impaired by alcohol, including judgment, reaction time, vision, and focus. Impaired driving includes driving without regard to your blood alcohol levels or exceeding the legal limits (**<u>80 milligrams of alcohol in 100 milliliters of blood or 0.08 for non-commercial vehicles</u>**) drug or marijuana consumption, a combination of both, refusing to obey police officer instructions to give a breath or blood sample, causing bodily damage or death and driving while your licence is suspended or disqualified for an impaired driving reason.

This limitation applies to numerous prescription medications and non-prescription cold and allergy solutions as well, as they can lead to impaired driving.

Driving in the State of North Carolina means automatically that **<u>the NCDMV has your full consent</u>** to test your blood breath or urine in case a law enforcement officer suspects that you are driving under the influence by signing your driver's licence, commonly referred to as the implied consent law.

The lawful age for purchasing alcoholic beverages in this state is 21. It is prohibited for individuals under the age of 21 to buy or attempt to purchase alcohol. hence, North Carolina has a zero-tolerance law, which means those **<u>under 21 drivers should have 0,00 BAC.</u>**

<u>An ignition interlock device</u> will be attached to the vehicle with a built-in breathalyzer to prevent the engine from starting if the driver is convicted of a DUI as a precautionary mechanism.

It is a common misconception that consuming water, coffee, or engaging in physical exercise can rapidly reduce blood alcohol content. In reality, these methods do not expedite the body's ability to metabolize alcohol.

The question is, is there any method that lowers your BAC after drinking? and the answer is that the only effective way to lower **BAC is to allow sufficient time** for the liver to process and eliminate alcohol from the bloodstream.

Not only that! The liver metabolizes alcohol **<u>at a relatively constant rate,</u>** and attempting to accelerate this process through hydration or exercise **does not** alter the body's natural detoxification timeline.

AUTO-INSURANCE

The state of North Carolina has a compulsory financial responsibility law requiring all vehicles registered in this state to **have auto liability insurance coverage.** The purpose of this law is to ensure that you can be financially responsible for any damages or injuries that occur in the event of an auto accident regardless of who is at fault.

This coverage pays for damages when accidentally injuring someone or damaging another vehicle or property in an auto accident. Keep in mind that this part of the policy only pays for the other person's injuries and damages to their vehicle and not your own.

The minimum liability insurance requirement is as follows:

- **$30,000** for bodily injury or death to one person in an accident.
- **$60,000** for bodily injury or death to two or more people in an accident.
- **$25,000** for property damage in an accident.

Evidence of financial responsibility, meanwhile, is required in the wake of an accident or law enforcement stop as proof that a motor vehicle owner has the means to pay for any damages/injuries that may have occurred. The most common form of said evidence? A liability insurance policy with at least the minimum required amount OR **standard proof** of liability insurance such as a certificate.

SAFETY BELT LAW

In the state of North Carolina, it is mandatory for all occupants in a vehicle to wear the required seat belt or restraint system that ensures their safety according to North Carolina laws and regulations.

Drivers with passengers under 16 must ensure that each of them is correctly secured either in a child passenger restraint system or a seat belt meeting applicable federal safety standards.

Age 8 and Younger, Weighing Less than 80 Pounds: Must be properly secured in a weight-appropriate child passenger restraint system.

Age 5 and Younger, Weighing Less than 40 Pounds (If the vehicle has an active passenger-side front airbag and a rear seat): Properly secured in the rear seat, unless the child restraint system is designed for front airbag use.

Age 8 and Weighing Between 40 and 80 Pounds (If no suitable seating positions with lap and shoulder belts are available): Can be restrained by a properly fitted lap belt only.

SPEED LAWS

In the state of North Carolina, speed limits are set by the Department of Transportation and enforced by law enforcement authorities. The speed limits are mostly displayed via signs along the roadway and are based on the type of road, vehicle, weather conditions and the surrounding area.

THE 4 MAJOR SPEED LAWS

The maximum speed law basically means you are not allowed to exceed the speed limit posted on a road sign. The following signs suggest different speed limits depending on the **location, type of vehicle, or time**.

The basic speed law is the most common of all and states that you should not exceed a safe speed on a roadway **based on weather and road conditions**. That being said, Speed restrictions indicate the fastest possible speed under ideal conditions, you must alter your driving speed in response to weather, road, and traffic circumstances. During rainy weather, for example, you should drive slower than the posted speed limit. The safest speed is one that gives you entire control of your car and allows you to avoid crashes.

The statutory or prima facie speed law mandates a statutory speed limit in areas where speed signs may not be posted, nevertheless, they should be known and followed by default.

The following are statutory speed limits :

*   **70mph** on Interstates
*   **55 mph** Outside towns/cities
*   **55 mph** on rural roads
*   **35 mph** in cities and towns.
*   **20 mph** in school zones when children are present

There is a law known as **the "Minimum Speed Regulation"** that requires drivers not to drive at a speed that is slower and excessively prudent, therefore it can impede, interrupt, or even block the normal flow of traffic.

When driving below the posted speed limit in multilane roads you must drive **in the right-hand lane.** Failure to follow this law can result in a traffic citation and fines.

Vice versa, the leftmost lane is dedicated to vehicles who want to **drive faster or pass** other vehicles while respecting the posted or statutory speed limit.

The Difference between these two Speed signs

Mandatory

Advisory

30

4 INTERSECTIONS AND LANE USAGE
Understanding The Dynamics of Different Types of
Intersections, lanes, and The Right of Way Rules

RIGHT-OF-WAY RULES

There is no denying the fact that there are high chances of collisions occurring at intersections, as we don't know who must move and who needs to yield. **The right-of-way** is a crucial rule that defines when and who should proceed first in such situations.

Rules of the road are generally established via signs, signals, and the location of your vehicle regarding other vehicles. Thus, the right-of-way rule requires one person to yield and allow the other to proceed following their position on the road.

Despite having the complete edge of the situation, you are still expected to demonstrate a responsible attitude by doing whatever it takes to avoid accidents. **A golden rule** is that the right-of-way is **always yielded, never seized**.

Directions and instructions **from a police officer** in an intersection or elsewhere **take precedence** over traffic signs or signals.

Throughout this chapter, we will explore the rules of right-of-way in **different scenarios**, including at intersections, during merging, and at roundabouts.

Driving at intersections is a very important component of the driving experience, this is because Intersections witness **a higher** **frequency of accidents** than any other location, and it's the one place where you're most likely to encounter and cross paths with vulnerable road users such as pedestrians, cyclists, motorcycle riders, scooters, and skaters.

INTERSECTIONS

An intersection is a point or area of the roadway where **two or more** roads converge, diverge, meet, or cross paths. It can take the form of a crossroad, commonly known as a four-way intersection or a T-junction or Y-junction in the case of three-way intersections, and vehicles need to interact with each other by stopping, yielding, or proceeding based on established traffic rules.

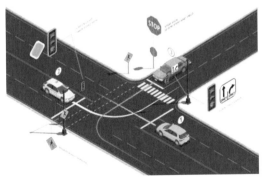

There are two types of intersections, the first one is a **controlled** intersection, meaning that it relies on traffic control signs and signals to control traffic flow. The second type is **uncontrolled** or blind intersections that use right-of-way rules for the same goal.

When a vehicle is about to turn on a roadway, common signs include **using signals, slowing down, and hesitating.** Pedestrians on the roadside may communicate to drivers that they intend to cross the street via eye contact or other nonverbal communication actions.

Traffic flow on the road

Blocking an intersection is generally considered to be a traffic violation as it can lead to traffic congestion and delays. In most jurisdictions in North America, it is illegal for a driver to enter an intersection if they **cannot clear it** before the traffic signal turns red or if traffic ahead of them stops.

The aim is to ensure that traffic can continue to flow smoothly and safely to prevent gridlock and to avoid compromising public safety, as such a situation can hinder the response time of emergency vehicles.

When an **emergency vehicle** is on its way and you're in an intersection hearing the siren of an emergency vehicle approaching, **never stop in an intersection, proceed through first**. then, pull over to the right at the earliest safe opportunity and come to a stop. Avoid making **sudden maneuvers** that could create further confusion or contribute to aggravating

the traffic congestion, and make sure your intentions are clear and communicated priorly via vehicle signals, hand signals, eye contact, or even verbal communication if the situation requires so.

When approaching an intersection, it is crucial to not only scan ahead but also check for cross traffic and pedestrians. Misjudging pedestrians can cause delays in the intersection and **lead to blockage as well**. Therefore, it's important to drive slowly, stay calm, and be able to interpret traffic patterns and predict the actions of other drivers.

CONTROLLED INTERSECTIONS

Controlled intersections **rely on stop signs, yield signs, and traffic lights** for traffic management.

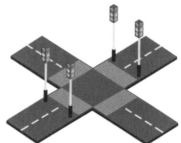

Controlled by a stoplight

In this case the right of way is determined by the stoplight. If you encounter a **stoplight**, and the light is currently green, you should be aware that it may turn yellow soon. If you're unable to stop safely because you are already too close to the intersection, you should **proceed through** with extreme caution.

If the light turns red while you are at the intersection, **stay calm and wait until there is sufficient space** to proceed in the direction you want to move to, but only when you are completely sure of completing the maneuver safely.

If you **plan to turn left** and face a long line of oncoming traffic, here's what you should do. When the light eventually turns green for both directions, position your front steering tires on the front crosswalk line and wait. Anticipate a gap in traffic, and after the opposite direction traffic clears, check your shoulder and make the left turn.

Controlled by a stop sign: Bring your vehicle to a complete stop, and if you can't see the cross-traffic or the intersection, then creep forward.

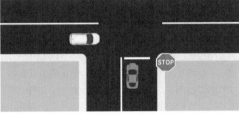

Stop completely at the indicated stop line. Wait until pedestrians can safely pass and the way is clear proceed

Do not cross a marked crosswalk when coming to a stop.

If there is no crosswalk or a stop line, stop before the intersecting roads at a distance of 10 feet.

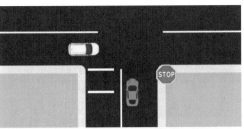

Note that there should be enough room (10 feet) for the pedestrians to walk by easily.

Two-way Stop sign intersection

You will most likely find a two-way stop sign intersection in the residential areas and there is going to be a major thoroughfare through those areas and all the minor roads must have stop signs. A two-way stop sign intersection is exactly as it sounds: in a four-way intersection, **two corners have** stop signs, while the other **two do not.** And it has different rules compared to the 3/4 way stop sign intersections. More particularly, the general rule of first to stop first to go **does not** apply here:

Hereby, the rules in this setup:

A. **Pedestrians first**
B. After that **major roads** have the right of way over **minor roads (or** the cross traffic who aren't controlled by a stop sign)
C. Straight through traffic over turning traffic
D. **Right-turning** over left-turning

Given this set-up, If two vehicles arrive and **they don't cross paths**, they can go **simultaneously**, for example, if they are both going straight from opposite directions or if one is going straight and the other is turning right.

Three and four way Stops intersections:

At a 3-way stop, also known as a T-intersection, all points of entry to the intersection must come to a complete stop before proceeding through. This rule applies not only to 3-way intersections but also to 4-way intersections and those with more points of entry.

When approaching a busy 4-way intersection, there are a few key pieces of information to keep in mind. Most 4-way stops have clearly marked stop lines, making it easy to know where to stop. In addition, because these intersections tend to be heavily trafficked, there are typically designated crosswalks for pedestrians.

Unlike a 2-way stop intersection, the right-of-way rule at a 3 and 4 ways stop is as follows *(See point B)*:

A. Pedestrians first
B. **followed by the first vehicle to arrive or stop, first to go.**
C. If two or more vehicles arrive simultaneously, the vehicle **on the right** has the right-of-way.
D. When it comes to turning, vehicles **going straight** have priority over turning vehicles.
E. If two vehicles are turning, the one making **a right turn** has the right-of-way over the one making a left turn.

"Courtesy corners" refer to intersections with stop signs on all corners. All four approaching vehicles arrive at the same time, this implies that there **is a car to everyone's right**, meaning that this situation can cause a confusion. In this case, either you or another driver should take the initiative by slightly moving forward and observing the other vehicle's reaction. If they give you the courtesy by letting you proceed, then the right-over-left vehicle rule applies to the rest of the vehicles at the intersection.

Controlled by a yield sign:

Yield signs mandate that drivers at intersections give the right of way to other road users already present, or alert drivers to approaching hazards.

When approaching a junction with a yield sign, drivers must come to a full stop and wait for any pedestrians or vehicles in the intersection to clear before proceeding. Yield signs are not commonly found in residential areas but are instead utilized in areas with lighter traffic flow and reduced collision risks.

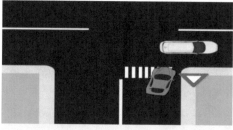

The right defensive position is to creep to the intersection to have a clear vision and to drive at a speed that permits you to stop with ease to prevent collisions.

UNCONTROLLED INTERSECTIONS

Uncontrolled or blind intersections are omnipresent in the quiet/residential areas where there is less volume of traffic. They can also be found in some industrial or rural zones. due to their unique nature, uncontrolled intersections have no traffic control signals or signs. You should scan the intersection very concisely to see if the other paths don't have any signs or lights.

The right-of-way rules in uncontrolled intersections **are exactly the same as in four-way** stop intersections:

In case you have reached an uncontrolled junction at the same time, the vehicle **that reached first** has the right of way over the vehicle arriving last.

If two vehicles arrive at the same time, the driver on the left must always yield to **the driver on the right**. However, the driver on the right must remain attentive to avoid any potential collisions.

Following traffic blindly at an intersection can be a dangerous habit. This can lead to an obstructed view by a large vehicle, truck, or commercial vehicle. Also, it may result in running a red light, causing potential accidents with cross traffic.

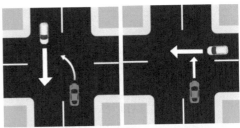

The blue car needs to yield to the **white car** in this case

The white car needs to yield to the **Blue car** in case of both paths in this T shaped intersection

Be extremely cautious in this situation as the drivers that are going straight through (white) make the assumption that they do have the right of way incorrectly.

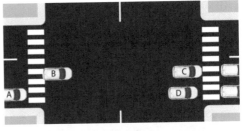

In this case, **A** is in the correct position. **B** has blocked the crosswalk. However, the **C & D** vehicles have used poor judgment

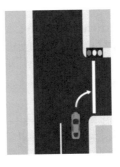

At pedestrian crossings and school crossings with a crosswalk, cede the right-of-way and wait for pedestrians to cross the road.

ROUNDABOUTS

 Roundabouts are circular forms of intersections, with vehicles traveling around a central island, they are specifically designed to enhance the safety and flow of traffic. And because vehicles can flow continuously through a roundabout, there are several benefits to that:

Firstly, there is often **less congestion and shorter delays** compared to normal intersections.

Secondly, **accidents** that do occur in roundabouts tend to be **less severe**, as vehicles are typically traveling at lower speeds and the circular design promotes more glancing blows rather than direct collisions.

And finally, **they can be adapted to various traffic conditions** and can accommodate different road users, including pedestrians and cyclists by relying on pedestrian crosswalks with refuge islands.

Vehicles that enter the roundabout should **yield to the traffic already in it.** In North America, traffic in roundabouts travels in a **counterclockwise direction.**

Nevertheless, in countries like the UK and Australia where they drive on the left side of the road traffic will flow in a clockwise direction, so be aware of that.

To navigate a roundabout safely and effectively, the recommended speed at the roundabout is **15 to 25 MPH.**

When exiting a roundabout, it's important to **signal your intention** to other drivers in advance to prevent accidents. For instance, if you are exiting from the left lane or making a U-turn, use your left turn signal to indicate your intention of turning left or making a U-turn.

Approach the exit with a reduced speed, ensuring you yield to any pedestrians in the crosswalk and **give priority to vehicles already within the roundabout**. Maintain a consistent speed as you navigate the exit curve. Always wait for a safe gap before merging into the next lane or onto the connecting road.

If you drive in a **multi-lane roundabout** you need to think of it as a conventional intersection. This means that every vehicle should travel in the appropriate lane based on its destination. To add that riders of motorcycles and bikes are entitled to use a full traffic lane.

More precisely, if you are traveling in **the right-hand lane**, your intention should be to make a **right turn or proceed straight through** the roundabout. Conversely, if you plan to make a U-turn or exit on the left, you should be in the left-hand lane.

Always be prepared to yield to vehicles **turning or exiting in front of you** from the inside as they have the right of way.

In a multi-lane roundabout, **do not overtake or attempt to overtake** because it can be a very dangerous maneuver. and only change lanes if road markings permit this action. Keep in mind that **predictability** is a key element when it comes to safety in roundabouts or intersections in general.

U- TURNS

U-turns are permitted only when they pose no danger to other road users. a common scenario that can make U-turns hazardous is executing them in locations **with limited visibility**, resulting in restrictions on such maneuvers.

These prohibited scenarios include: near the crest of hills or curves, interstate highways, busy business districts, whenever a no U-turn sign or signal is displayed, in the presence of solid white or yellow pavement marking on your side of the roadway, in an intersection controlled by a police officer, or any other situation where you or other motorists cannot see **500 feet away.**

When U-turns are allowed, visibility is clear but the road is narrow, you should perform a **3-point U-turn.**

If you happen to **miss your exit** on a freeway or highway**, never attempt to stop, back up, or make a U-turn.**

Here is how you can execute a 3 point U-turn:

A. Move as far right as possible, check traffic carefully, then use your left turn signal, Rotate the steering wheel to the left, and proceed forward at a slow pace.
B. Come to a halt at the curb or edge of the roadway. Transition to reverse, turn the wheels sharply to the right, verify traffic, and reverse your vehicle
C. By then, lightly adjust your steering wheel to the direction where you aim to go

MERGING LANES

Changing lanes is a very important component of defensive driving. Understand that when you move from one marked lane to another, you are required to give the right of way to the vehicles that are **already in that particular lane.** This applies to all situations, including when you are merging into a freeway.

To switch lanes safely, you must use your vehicle's signals to indicate your intention to change lanes and only make the move when there is a safe gap in the traffic.

Before accessing a highway or freeway, check for cross traffic and turn onto the acceleration lane. You are not considered to be on the acceleration lane until you pass the continuity lines.

Zip merging is when 2 lanes of traffic merge into one, on a road where there is no road marking, giving the right of way to any vehicle which has any part of its vehicle ahead of yours.

When merging back into traffic **after an emergency stop,** proceed with caution and observe your surroundings. Before attempting to merge, check your mirrors, and blind spots, and scan the road for any oncoming vehicles. Always signal your intention to merge by using your turn signal.

Tailgating means driving too closely to the vehicle in front, therefore it is an extremely dangerous behavior on the road. When a driver tailgates, they leave little to no space to react in case the vehicle in front suddenly brakes or swerves. This greatly increases the risk of rear-ending the vehicle in front, which can result in serious injuries or even fatalities. Tailgating is also a traffic infraction, prohibited in all North American jurisdictions, and can result in hefty penalties and demerit points.

LANE MANAGEMENT

A key element to ensuring safety at intersections **is proper lane positioning** before making a turn. Being positioned in the correct lane well before entering an intersection allows for smooth and predictable traffic flow, and reduces the likelihood of last-minute maneuvers. This means that you should use the leftmost lane when making a left turn or U-turn, the middle lanes when going straight through, and the rightmost lane when turning right.

Pay attention to these lane control signs as they indicate **the direction specific lanes should follow**

For brand-new drivers, when and how to perform a shoulder check may pose a challenge, first of all, shoulder checks are an essential way to look for vehicles coming from behind and to check **for blind spots** while changing lanes, making a turn, or merging with existing traffic roadway, the technic is simple, quickly glance over your shoulder while having a safe following distance.

One of the most important rules of driving is to **never change lanes in an intersection.** This is because making sudden turns through an intersection or roundabout (which is also considered an intersection) makes you unpredictable and goes against safe driving practices. Even if there is no legislation presented for it, make sure to never change lanes in an intersection, as it significantly increases the chance of being involved in a risky situation.

When driving on **high-speed roads** such as interstates or freeways, you are required to use **the rightmost lane** in case you want to travel **slower than the flow of traffic**, and vice versa, if you decide to drive **faster,** but never above the posted or statutory speed limit, **the leftmost lane** is dedicated to that.

Numerous road users utilize North Carolina roadways, including pedestrians, motorcyclists, cyclists, large trucks, buses, and agricultural equipment. This means that each of them requires specific precautionary measures for the safety and comfort of all.

SHARING THE ROAD WITH OTHER ROAD USERS

PEDESTRIANS :

When it comes to crosswalks or intersections, pedestrians **have the right-of-way first at all times**.

Controlled intersections via a traffic light require pedestrians to give way when the light is green. Nevertheless, drivers need to always be cautious and give the way even if the light is green if a pedestrian is nonchalant about traffic rules, or if the light turned green while the pedestrian is on his way to complete the crosswalk.

A Right turn on red requires the driver **to stop**, check for traffic left and right, give way to pedestrians, and allow them ample time to cross.

Another **key element** to pedestrian safety is **eye contact** between both the pedestrian and the vehicle.

As a driver, it is important to know that stopping on the pedestrian crosswalk **is strictly illegal** as it forces pedestrians to walk around your vehicle out into moving traffic. Which puts their life in danger and makes them less visible for oncoming traffic.

Pay attention to pedestrians **at the edge of the crosswalk** getting ready to enter or from the other side of the street crossing. You still need to slow down and stop for pedestrians in the opposite direction of traffic.

When driving in residential areas or school zones, keep in mind that **children and youngsters are unpredictable and they** might **follow a ball** that is bouncing into the road. Use the same caution and consideration when a pedestrian is elderly or disabled, as they need more time to cross the street.

When nearing a **stationary vehicle** from the rear, reduce your speed and refrain from overtaking until you are certain there are no pedestrians in front.

Reminder: **Blind** or **visually impaired** pedestrians can use a **white cane** or a **guiding dog** to help them cross intersections.

BICYCLISTS

With the pleasant weather, the influx of bicycles and cyclists is inevitable and not all cyclists opt for helmets or reflective gear, making them potentially harder to notice. however, you should be on the lookout for those vulnerable road users and give them enough room so they can operate safely on the road.

As a vehicle driver, you need to understand well that not all bicyclists or riders have **the same skill level.** Therefore, some of them might be unpredictable.

In North Carolina's highways, **a 4- feet minimum distance i**s required between vehicles and bicyclists.

Indeed, bicyclists are legal drivers with laws and regulations established for their use. Sharing the road with them means mutual respect which can be promoted by public information.

Follow the instructions below:

A. Yield to bicycles when turning.
B. Always give bicyclists more passing room in adverse weather
C. Make a visual check for bikes by checking mirrors and using shoulder checks before you enter or leave any lane of traffic.
D. Reduce your speed when passing bikes when the road is narrow.
E. Don't use your horn at bicyclists it can cause them to swerve into traffic or off the road.

MOTORCYCLISTS

Because of their dimensions, motorcycles can be hard to see or can hide in your blind spots, especially at night, in bad weather, or in heavy traffic. They are also more prone to injury in a collision because they are less guarded.

You need also to allow **at least four to five seconds** of **following distance** when you are behind a motorcycle. Be cautious motorcycles are closer than they seem. And because of their smaller size, they may be harder to spot on your blind spots. And, same as cars, motorcycles are allowed **an entire lane**.

When motorbikes are slowing down they may use their throttle instead of their brake, so you may **not see the brake lights.** You need also to know that road conditions affect their driving differently such as uneven pavement and slippery roads.

Driving a quiet vehicle: Operators hybrid and electric cars should be aware that persons with low eyesight often depend on the sounds of an engine before approaching an intersection. Because a hybrid or electric car produces little or no perceptible noise while slowing or stopping.

COMMERCIAL VEHICLES

Driving safely in the presence of large commercial vehicles and eventually avoiding collision is the product of being familiar with their physical capabilities and maneuvers. Large commercial vehicles are designated to transport cargo and are not as maneuverable as passenger vehicles.

Large trucks have **longer stopping distances,** they take more space for turns and they weigh more. They also have **wider blind spots** to which your vehicle can get lost, the blind spots or no zone areas are: **directly in front, directly behind, and along each side**.

You need to be careful of all large heavy vehicles **that are turning**, they cannot see cars directly behind or beside them, and they may need to **use multiple lanes** to navigate turns safely. Never linger alongside a truck while passing, try to escape by passing the truck, or if it's not possible back off. pass or overtake a truck with care.

Try not to pass or overtake a truck on the left-hand side, this is because a truck blind spot on the left runs down the left of the trailer and extends out three lanes. for all turning vehicles the rear wheels follow a shorter path than the front wheels. Therefore, truck drivers frequently need to make wide turns when executing a right or left maneuver.

Ensure you can see the driver in their **side mirrors**; if you can't, they likely can't see you.

Always give room for doubt, if you think the truck is turning right wait a second and check the turning signals again the driver may be turning left. Also, avoid passing a turning truck or bus on the right, as they make wide turns that can pose a risk to vehicles on their right side.

Large commercial vehicles need a **significantly larger braking distance** than regular vehicles. When overtaking a huge vehicle, avoid getting in front of it. This is not only impolite, but it is also hazardous since it increases the safe distance required for huge cars to brake in time.

FLASHING LIGHTS SCHOOL BUS

When a stopped school bus has its red or amber lights flashing, **stop** regardless of being behind the bus or approaching it from the front. Considering that the bus is in front of you, stop at a **safe distance** to allow children to leave and cross the road ahead.

For those approaching it from behind, ensure that you stop at a distance of **at least 10 feet** and wait until the bus has moved or its lights stopped flashing before continuing your journey. Only traffic coming from the rear must stop if a **median strip** is separating the road.

A stop sign arm is used on the driver's side of school buses. This arm extends out once the red lights start to flash, and it resembles a typical stop sign.

THE TWO-SECOND RULE

Maintaining a safe distance between vehicles while driving is critical to help prevent rear-end collisions, as following too closely behind another vehicle (i.e., tailgating) is a serious infraction that can lead to the same.

To avoid finding yourself in a (eek) rear-end collision with another vehicle, obey **the "Two-second rule"**: a principal that encourages drivers to maintain a safe distance between themselves and the vehicle in front of them by adhering to a gap of (yes) at **least 2 seconds**. This amount of time can allow for a safe stopping distance in case of sudden braking or an emergency of some type. Keep in mind this "rule" is subject to change depending on road conditions, weather, and traffic density: meaning sometimes additional reaction time is necessary.

ENTERING A HIGHWAY

All entrances to limited access highways are comprised of three essential parts, **namely an entrance ramp, an acceleration lane, and a merging area.**

At the entrance ramp, you should start looking for an opening and signal your intention to merge onto the highway. As the ramp straightens into the acceleration lane, increase your speed and adjust it accordingly to merge into traffic when you reach the end of the acceleration lane.

Once you are in the merging area, yield to traffic already on the highway.

When leaving a limited-access highway, get into the rightmost lane. Always use your turning signals to indicate your intention to exit, and as you approach the exit ramp, slow down in the deceleration lane.

PASSING OTHER VEHICLES

Passing is a crucial part of the driving experience, and it can be done both safely or in an illegal way that endangers other road users. Passing is always **allowed on the left** as long as you respect the rules of the road and you can execute the passing safely. The steps of safe passing are:

A. Check if there is a sign, signal, or pavement marking that prohibits passing
B. Check your mirrors first and make sure you have enough room to complete the maneuver
C. Signal your intentions via vehicle turning signals or hand turning signal
D. Change your lane smoothly and enter the passing lane
E. Accelerate to a speed that allows passing and return to your original lane when you can see the passed vehicle's headlights in your rearview mirror

While **passing on the right is generally prohibited,** it is permissible if the roadway is unobstructed and wide enough for multiple lanes of traffic. You can also pass on the right when the vehicle being overtaken **is either making or about to make a left turn or is on a one-way street**

42

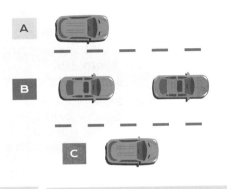

A	REARVIEW MIRROR
B	DRIVER MIRROR
C	BLIND POINT

SLOW MOVING VEHICLES

The slow moving vehicle sign is an orange triangle in the center and red on the borders. And it is more present in industrial and rural areas. The slow moving vehicles sign is for vehicles that are doing **less than 25 MPH**.

CAUTION
SLOW MOVING
VEHICLES

Slow-moving vehicles can be either farm equipment, horse-drawn vehicles if you are in an industrial area these will be the industrial equipment, or if you are around a marine environment another type of slow-moving vehicle will be there, and you will need to know how to handle this and identify this sign.

Sometimes vehicles with that sign move over to the shoulder of the road and sometimes they don't. If they stay on the roadway, you will have to pass, and you need to be careful when you are passing because it is one of the highest-risk crashes. Take into consideration

road markings as well, they will give you an indication of whether it is safe to pass or not. If you are not comfortable with the gap, work with a veteran driver who can help you out with judging the gap to be able to pass safely.

Following traffic blindly is a dangerous habit. This can lead to an obstructed view by a large vehicle. Also, it may result in running a red light, causing potential accidents with cross traffic.

FUNERAL PROCESSION

If you see a funeral procession on the road, **Give them the way and yield**, you should not cut in and out. All vehicles in question must have their emergency flashers and headlights on to indicate their inclusion in the procession.

Drivers within funeral processions can move through a stop sign or a red traffic light if the leading vehicle does so while the traffic light is green. Nevertheless, Funeral processions **must always yield to emergency vehicles**.

STOPPING DISTANCE

Your stopping distance is the distance a vehicle travels from the moment a driver perceives the need to stop until the vehicle comes to a complete halt. In many cases, drivers do not realize how long it takes to stop while traveling at a certain speed.

Calculating stopping distance :

Stopping distances can come in a matter of seconds that determine if you will be able to stop or not in time of hazard. It is a better practice to calculate the distance and time required to stop the vehicle.

This practice can reduce the risk of an accident if made correctly while getting more experienced as a driver this will become a second nature, that's why experienced drivers brake on time.

<u>**You can estimate the elements that enable a total stopping distance via this formula :**</u>

	Perception distance
+	**Reaction distance**
+	**Braking distance**

= TOTAL STOPPING DISTANCE

<u>Perception time </u>is the time it takes a driver to understand a situation and realize he needs to stop. Human judgment upon encountering a hazardous situation varies from one person to another. Drivers need **around 1.5 seconds** to observe a hazard and acknowledge its presence.

Nevertheless, eye health, exhaustion, and impaired driving can **increase** your perception time.

<u>Reaction time </u>is based on human reflexes and quick judgment upon encountering hazardous situations. On average, a driver requires about **one second** to initiate a physical response, lifting their foot off the accelerator and applying the brakes.

However, distractions, inexperience, driving under the influence of drugs or alcohol, and exhaustion can **increase** reaction time.

<u>Braking time,</u> A vehicle's braking time is determined by the time it takes the vehicle to stop once applying the brakes. The total distance traveled by the vehicle during this time period is considered as the **braking distance**. The speed of traveling, the condition of your vehicle tires, the weather, and the road play a major role in extending the braking time. Your tires affect your vehicle's stopping distance. Measure both the pressure and tread depth regularly and before long journeys. Always remember that **<u>When stopping, you should begin braking early.</u>**

DRIVING IN LOW VISIBILITY CONDITIONS

Driving during the day in comparison to driving at night poses distinct challenges and differences primarily due to variations in visibility, lighting conditions, and potential hazards.

In the state of North Carolina, make sure to switch on your headlights between **sunset and sunrise,** and at any other time when **visibility is low 400 feet or less**.

<u>OVERDRIVING YOUR HEADLIGHTS</u>

When you drive so quickly that your stopping distance is greater than what your headlights can see, you are overdriving your headlights.

This is a risky maneuver since you may not leave yourself enough space to come to a safe halt. Reflective road signs might also deceive you by making you assume you can see further than you actually can. If you are not careful, you may over-drive your headlights.

TURN ON HEADLIGHTS

Turning on **the high beam** will significantly improve your visibility, but they are only appropriate on roads with **low or regular oncoming traffic**.

They **must be switched off** to prevent you from dazzling other drivers in **concentrated areas** such as towns and cities that have street lighting and here you do not need to use high beams.

When driving on sunny days or in situations where other drivers have not been considerate and use their high beams then perform the following steps. Look downwards towards the **right side** of the road. **Focus on the edge of the lane** and avoid looking directly ahead until the vehicle or sun glare passes.

LOWBEAM HEADLIGHTS

First, there are low-beam headlights. These are located at the front of the vehicle and are used most during the night. They point downwards which is why they are also called "dipped headlights", in essence, they reduce the possibility of dazzling other drivers at night. You may also use them whenever visibility is low.

FOG LIGHTS

Front and rear fog lights help drivers see better in **adverse weather.** Not all vehicles are equipped with front fog lights, but nearly all vehicles have rear fog lights installed. Front fog lights are located on the lowest front bumper and come in pairs. A fog light

switch is found inside the cabin and can be switched on **during foggy weather** or where there is rain or heavy mist. They should however be switched off when the visibility has improved, as there is a risk of dazzling other drivers.

HIGHBEAM HEADLIGHTS

Full-beam headlights give drivers the most visibility in nighttime conditions or unlit areas. They light straight ahead instead of pointing downwards and only should be used when the road is not lit by street lights. All drivers are required to dim their headlights **within 500 feet of an oncoming vehicle**, which is approximately "one block", and **300 feet when following** another vehicle.

EMERGENCY FLASHERS

When you switch on your emergency lights, all four turning lights illuminate at the same time in a repeated rhythm. But the emergency lights should only be used in the following situations: If your vehicle is not working as it should. You need to pull over, switching your emergency lights on will show other road users that you **have an emergency** and It will allow other drivers to see you from a distance, so **they can plan** their next move.

Another situation for emergency lights in some states (when allowed) is during **a funeral procession**. Often funerals use slow-moving vehicles, and the emergency lights warn other drivers about the procession.

TURNING LIGHTS

 Your turning lights are used when you want to turn left or right. They are located on each corner of the vehicle, with some models having additional turning lights on the wings or mirrors. Their primary function is to tell other people (drivers and pedestrians) that you are turning left or right soon. This allows other drivers to **adjust their position** accordingly.

Ensure that you use your turning lights **within 100 feet** of executing the maneuver. Too early may mean that you are informing drivers of a closer turning than intended, too late and other drivers **will not have enough time to react** or know what your next move will be.

YOUR TIRE'S CONDITION

Sometimes a tire can blow which could be alarming. The signs that your tire has blown include **shaking of the vehicle, sudden loud noise**, and the vehicle generally becomes hard to drive. A driver should take extra caution with steering and focus on **driving in a straight line** as much as possible. Then slowly take your foot off the accelerator to slow down carefully. Turn on your emergency lights to inform other drivers that you will be stopping soon, and steer into the right lane, pulling over as soon as it is safe.

Inspecting your tires regularly for wear is vital to ensure your vehicle is safe. Sometimes you may experience a **shaking steering wheel** when driving **at higher speeds**. This could indicate an **unbalanced wheel**. Every time a tire is replaced, the technician will use a wheel balancing machine to ensure the rotation of the wheel is smooth. The machine will inform the technician that a weight is needed to balance the wheel rotation and ensure your vehicle drives smoothly.

when a vehicle's tires lose traction with the road surface, **this is called a skid**, and the common causes of skidding are sudden acceleration or deceleration, harsh braking when the roadway is wet, and sharp turns at a high speed, when this happens, you can recover by Steering in the direction you want to go and easing off the accelerator and braking gently.

Regularly inspecting your tires and checking for damage, uneven wear, and cracks is important as any damage could cause problems when braking or during harsh cornering

If the vehicle's tire pressure is too low, then it's harder to steer and avoid objects. If it's too high then less rubber is in contact with the road. Both under and over-pressured tires will increase your stopping distance.

Sometimes these weights can be incorrect or simply fall off when driving. **Causing an imbalance**. When this occurs, take your vehicle into a workshop for inspection. The technician can take a look at all four wheels and the suspension system to diagnose the fault and recommend steps to fix it.

6

Section 1
Road signs

Q1/ This Traffic Sign Indicates That:

1- No left turn is allowed
2- U-Turn is not allowed
3- A U-Turn is allowed only if there is no traffic jam

Q2/ This Traffic Sign Indicates That:

1- Children are playing in a residential area and to drive safely
2- You are entering a school zone
3- Direction sign for employees

Q3/This Traffic Sign Indicates:

1- A housing Area
2- A helicopter Airport
3- A hospital

Q4/ This Traffic Sign Indicates That:

1- No bicycles are authorized on this road at any time
2- Do not stand or stop in this area
3- School area

Q5/ This Traffic Sign Indicates That:

1- A Zoo is ahead
2- Hunting animals is permitted in this area
3- Deer regularly cross, be alert for animals

Q6/ This Traffic Sign Indicates That:

1- A road turns right then left
2- You need to keep right of the obstacle (median, traffic island, etc.)
3- A winding road is ahead

Q7/ This Traffic Sign Indicates That:

1- You cannot enter
2- An uncontrolled intersection is ahead
3- A railroad crossing is ahead

Q8/ This Traffic Sign Indicates:

1- A regulatory sign
2- A warning sign
3- A sign for temporary conditions

Q9/ This Traffic Sign Indicates That:

1- Workers on the road ahead symbol
2- This is a construction sign, slow down and obey the flagman's direction
3- A construction sign replacing flagman on duty

Q10/ This Traffic Sign Indicates:

1- Drive to the right
2- Right turn yield
3- Slower traffic should move to the right

Q11/ This Traffic Sign Indicate:

1- No parking is allowed starting at the arrows to the corner
2- A lane usage road sign authorizing right turn only
3- A lane usage road sign allowing all turns

Q12/ This Traffic Sign Indicates That:

1- A stop sign is located 100 feet ahead
2- A bump is located 100 feet ahead
3- A stoplight is ahead

Q13/ This Traffic Sign Indicates That:

1- Bicycles are authorized on this road
2- No bicycles are allowed on this road
3- Vehicle stopping is not allowed

Q14/ This Traffic Sign Indicates That:

1- A stop sign is ahead, slow down, drive through the junction with caution if you see other vehicles
2- You need to slow down, if it's necessary, yield right of way to approaching vehicles
3- You should stop and yield the right-of-way to passing vehicles from both directions

Q15/ This Traffic Sign Indicates That:

1- Slippery conditions occur when wet
2- You will share the road with oncoming traffic
3- You need to drive with caution

Q16/ This Traffic Sign Indicates That:

1- An intersection is ahead
2- A narrow road is ahead
3- A railway crossing is ahead

Q17/ This Traffic Sign Indicates:

1- Route to airport
2- Air show ahead
3- Airplane landing

Q18/ This Traffic Sign Indicates That:

1- Speed limit on a route
2- Us numbered route sign
3- Speed limit on a highway

Q19/ This Traffic Sign Indicates That:

1- Alert slow-moving vehicle
2- A dead-end street is ahead
3- Yield to traffic at the intersection

Q20/ This Traffic Sign Indicates That:

1- Pavement is grooved
2- Construction zone
3- No passing

Q21/ This Traffic Sign Indicates That:

1- An intersection is straight ahead
2- A right turn is not allowed
3- Driving straight through the intersection isn't permitted

Q22/ This Traffic Sign Indicates That:

1- The road ahead is separated by a median; keep to the right
2- A narrow bridge is ahead
3- A divided highway begins

Q23/ This Traffic Sign Indicates That:

1- No passing
2- This sign is temporarily
3- All of the above

Q24/ This Traffic Sign Indicates:

1- A direction to nearby towns and cities
2- An upcoming roundabout and information about directions
3- Distances to neighbouring towns

Q25/ This Traffic Sign Indicates That:

1- You should not take the right-hand lane under any circumstances
2- An end of the highway is ahead you need to move to the right lane
3- Two way left turn lane

Q26/ This Traffic Sign Indicates That:

1- Uneven pavement is ahead
2- Railroad crossing is ahead
3- No vehicles on train track

Q27/ This Traffic Sign Indicates That:

1- A school zone area
2- A pedestrian crosswalk
3- Rest area ahead

Q28/ This Traffic Sign Indicates That:

1- Electric charging vehicle station
2- Electric charging phone station
3- Fuel station

Q25/ This Traffic Sign Indicates That:

1- No U-turns are allowed
2- A hidden intersection is ahead
3- Lane merging from the right side, vehicles coming from both roads are equally responsible to merge correctly

Q30/ This Traffic Sign Indicate:

1- No Littering is allowed
2- A Ramp is closed
3- No Hitchhiking

Q31/ Does This Traffic Sign Indicates That :

1- *The Pavement narrows ahead, drive safely*
2- *A right lane end is ahead; in case you drive In the right lane, you need to merge with traffic into the left*
3- *Divided highway ends, you should know that traffic travels in both directions*

Q33/ This Traffic Sign Indicates That:

1- *Roundabout ahead*
2- *Do not enter this road*
3- *Closed road due to construction*

Q35/ This Traffic Sign Indicates That:

1- *You must turn right*
2- *Traffic may only travel in one direction*
3- *Keep to the right of the traffic island*

Q37/ This Traffic Sign Indicates That:

1- *A road becomes slippery when wet*
2- *A winding road is ahead*
3- *A narrow road is ahead*

Q39/ This Traffic Sign Indicates That:

1- *Reserved lane for disabled persons*
2- *Disabeled person parking*
3- *You can park only for 30 minutes*

Q32/ This Traffic Sign Indicates That:

1- *A narrow road*
2- *A temporarily closed road*
3- *Drawbridge ahead (Bridge that lifts or swings to allow boats to pass)*

Q34/ This Traffic Sign Indicates That:

1- *The ending of a high occupency vehicle lane*
2- *HOV lane is ahead*
3- *Two way left turn ends*

Q36/ This Traffic Sign Indicates That:

1- *You may not park between the signs during the posted time*
2- *No parking at any time in this area*
3- *You may park in this area during the announced time*

Q38/ This Traffic Sign Indicates:

1- *The maximum speed at night is 25 MPH*
2- *The maximum speed on roadway is 25 MPH*
3- *A maximum speed limit is determined on the curve*

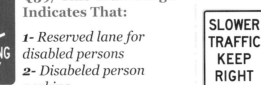

Q40/ Does This Traffic Sign Indicates That :

1- *Drive to the right*
2- *Right turn yield*
3- *Slower traffic you need to keep or move to the right*

Q41/ This Traffic Sign Indicates That:

1- No parking is allowed 5.4m from here
2- A winding road ahead
3- Underpass ahead. Take caution if your vehicle is over 12.6"

Q42/ This Traffic Sign Indicates The:

1- End of a 50 mph zone
2- the maximum speed allowed in the curve is 50MPH
3- Speed limit will change to a maximum speed of 50 MPH

Q43/ This Traffic Sign Indicates That:

1- No right turns on red
2- Right turn allowed on red
3- No right turn is permitted

Q44/ Does This Traffic Sign Indicates That :

1- A divided highway begins
2- A divided highways ends
3- A bumpy road is ahead

Q45/ Does This Traffic Sign Indicates That :

1- Do not enter the port area
2- Fire hall
3- There may be water flowing over the road

Q46/ This Traffic Sign Indicates That:

1- Parking is not authorized
2- A hazard sign, the downward line reveals the side on which you can safely pass
3- Roundabout ahead drive responsibly

Q47/This Traffic Sign Indicates:

1- A permissive sign
2- A truck route
3- Dangerous goods road

Q48/ This Traffic Sign Indicates That:

1- Multiple roundabouts are ahead
2- A roundabout is ahead
3- A road is separated by a median

Q49/ This Traffic Sign Indicates That:

1- The two left lanes ahead are closed
2- There is a highway with 2 left lanes ahead
3- Two or more passengers in the vehicle are required to take the left lane

Q50/ This Traffic Sign Indicates that:

1- You are coming to school zone area with plenty of school buses
2- You are coming to a bus station
3- You are coming to a rail station

Q51/ This Traffic Sign Indicates That:

1- Watch for children crosswalk
2- During school hours and when the yellow lights are flashing obey the maximum speed limits as mentioned on the sign
4- Watch for pedestrians to drive safely at a maximum speed of 20 MPH

Q53/ This Traffic Sign Indicates That:

1- The road will end ahead, you must turn to the left road
2-There is a sharp bend or turn ahead
3- You must keep to the left, traffic must exist

Q55/ This Traffic Sign Indicates That:

1- A right lane will end ahead
2- Passing is strictly not allowed
3- Parking is strictly not allowed

Q57/ This Traffic Sign Indicates:

1- A rural region
2- A railway crossing
3- A pharmacy sign

Q59/ This Traffic Sign Indicates That:

1- A railroad crossing is ahead
2- A four-way road is ahead
3- An intersection is ahead

Q52/ This Traffic Sign Indicates That:

1- You should not stop in the space between the signs
2- You should not park in the space between the signs
3- Dangerous goods aren't allowed on this route

Q52/ This Traffic Sign Indicates That:

1- An Intersection ahead
2- A sideroad ahead
3- A sharp bend on right

Q56/ This Traffic Sign Indicates That:

1- Bumpy road
2- Large trucks should drive at 8% of the normal speed limit
3- Steep hill is ahead

Q58/ This Traffic Sign Indicates That:

1- A pedestrian crosswalk
2- A survey crew working
3- A person who controls the traffic is ahead

Q60/ This Traffic Sign Indicates :

1- The recommended following distance at night
2- The maximum speed limit at night
3- The lawful following distance at night

Q61/ This Traffic Sign Indicates That:

1- Road ends ahead
2- A roundabout is ahead
3- A stop sign is ahead

Q63/ This Traffic Sign Indicates That:

1- You are not allowed to go straight, only left or right turns
2- You can only go straight in the intersection ahead
3- Route ends ahead

Q65/ Does This Traffic Sign Indicates That :

1- Police, mobile radar detector ahead
2- A Survey crew working on the road ahead
3- An officer who manages traffic is ahead, follow his instructions. Slowly and watch for the instructions

Q67/ This Traffic Sign Indicates That:

1- Snow may be in this area, drive responsibly
2- Road becomes slippery when wet
3- Mountains ahead

Q69/ This Traffic Sign Indicates That:

1- Road forks to the right
2- A highway exit
3- You must turn right, the road ends ahead

Q62/ This Traffic Sign Indicates That:

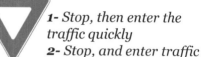

1- Stop, then enter the traffic quickly
2- Stop, and enter traffic slowly
3- Slow down, stop if necessary, and yield the right of way

Q64/ This Traffic Sign Indicates That:

1- Keep to the left
2- This is a guide for drivers in order to warn you of a change in direction
3- You are asked to stay to the right of the centre island

Q66/ This Traffic Sign Indicates That:

1- Bumpy road ahead
2- Risk of falling rocks
3- Mountains ahead

Q68/ This Traffic Sign Indicates That:

1- Allow space between your vehicle and cyclists
2- No motorists are allowed
3- No buses or trucks are allowed

Q70/ This Traffic Sign Indicates That:

1- A divided highway begins
2- An interstate highway marker
3- Interchange direction sign

Q71/ Does This Traffic Sign Indicates That :

1- You will need to share the road with motorists, Thus providing some space
2- This is a guide for drivers to pass the sharp curves safely
3- The left lane ahead is closed due to roadwork. respect the speed limitation and merge safely with traffic

Q72/ This Traffic Sign Indicates That:

1- Bicycle crossing ahead or bicycle usually use this road
2- Bicycles aren't allowed
3- Bicycles are temporarily not allowed

Q73/ This Traffic Sign Indicates :

1- An X intersection is ahead
2- A crossroad is ahead
3- A railroad crossing is ahead

Q74/ This Traffic Sign Indicates That:

1- Heavy trucks are allowed on this road
2- Heavy trucks aren't allowed on this roadway
3- Road for trucks only

Q75/ This Traffic Sign Indicates That:

1- Construction zone ahead
2- A route to avoid a construction zone or even a severe traffic collision
3- A roundabout exit

Q76/ This Traffic Sign Indicates :

1- An interstate highway marker
2- The maximum speed limit in the interstate highway is 22 MPH
3- The number of miles until the interstate exit

Q77/ This Traffic Signal Indicates that:

1- A Light rail is activated
2- A railroad crossing
3- You are not allowed to drive on the rails track

Q78/ What does this road sign mean?

1- A T-intersection ahead, you can only turn right or left
2- The rails of a narrow bridge are ahead
3- The road is closed ahead

Q79/ This Traffic Sign Indicates That:

1- Pedestrians aren't allowed
2- Pedestrians are permitted
3- A crosswalk is ahead

Q80/ Does This Traffic Sign Indicates That :

1- A highway is ahead
2- Road sharply curves right then left
3- Road curves right then left

Q81/ This Traffic Sign Indicates That:

1- Multiple roundabouts ahead
2- Narrow road ahead
3- Road is separated by a median

Q82/ This Traffic Sign Indicates That:

1- Left turn is not allowed, you must turn right
2- Left turn is not allowed at the intersection ahead
3- No left turn on all the upcoming intersections

Q83/ This Traffic Sign Indicates:

1- Facilities that are accessible for disabled persons
2- Yield right of way to those with special needs
3- An exclusive lane for disabled persons

Q84/ Does This Traffic Sign Indicates That :

1- Don't pass the pilot vehicle and don't pace the vehicle bearing this traffic sign
2- Cars are not allowed in this lane
3- When flashing, you are advised to keep to the right and drive responsibly

Q85/ This Traffic Sign Indicates That:

1- A Winding road is ahead
2- The road ahead sharply turn left then right
3- The road ahead sharply turn right then left

Q86/ This Traffic Sign Indicates That:

1- You are allowed to park in this space
2- You are allowed to park only for 30 min
3- Weekend parking is for fully licensed drivers

Q87/ This Traffic Sign Indicates That:

1- No littering
2- No texting
3- No hitchhiking

Q88/ This Sign is :

1- A yield sign
2- A stop sign
3- A warning sign

Q89/ This Traffic Sign Indicates That:

1- Advisory Speed Limit in the curve
2- Advisory Speed Limit temporarily on a construction area
3- Advisory Speed Limit in a school zone

Q90/ This Traffic Sign Indicates That:

1- A temporary winding road
2- A detour from the traffic route is ahead
3- Sharp curve is ahead

Q91/ This Traffic Sign Indicates That:

1- Flashing lights on the arrows show the direction of an exit
2- Flashing lights on the arrows show the direction to follow
3- Traffic keep left

Q92/ This Traffic Sign Indicates That:

1- No parking between signs includes all types of vehicles
2- You cannot stop your vehicle in this area unless you need to load or unload a passenger or merchandise
3- All answers above are correct

Q93/ This Traffic Sign Indicates:

1- A museem for us history is ahead
2- A network of highway across our country
3- A highway marker sign

Q94/ This Traffic Sign Indicates That:

1- A divided highway begins
2- Merging traffic from both sides
3- Traffic may pass the obstruction on left or right

Q95/ This Traffic Sign Indicates That:

1- lanes reserved for vehicles with one passenger only
2- Bicycles are not permitted
3- Special vehicles may take this lane either at all times or during certain hours

Q96/ This Traffic Sign Indicates That:

1- You are allowed to only park in this space during the times mentioned
2- You are not allowed to turn left during the times shown bellow
3- You are not allowed to make a U-turn during the times shown bellow

Q97/ This Traffic Sign Indicates :

1- Chevron alignment
2- That you must keep right
3- The direction you must follow at a roundabout

Q98/ Does This Traffic Sign Indicates That :

1- Never drive past this sign
2- Paved road ends ahead
3- A dead end ahead

Q99/ This Traffic Sign Indicates That:

1- Offset side roads are ahead
2- Warning of one way roads
3- Hazardous roadway warning

Q100/ This Traffic Sign Indicates That:

1- Vaccine centre
2- Emergency medical services
3- Hospital

Q101/ Does This Traffic Sign Indicates That :

1- You are allowed to only park in this space during the times mentioned
2- You are allowed to park only for 1 hour
3- Weekend parking is for fully licensed drivers

Q102/ This Traffic Sign Indicates That:

1- You are coming to a pedestrian crossing, yield the right of way
2- When turning yield to pedestrians
3- Turning on green isn't allowed

Q133/ This Traffic Sign Indicates That:

1- A paved surface ends ahead
2- Do not block the intersection
3- Watch for falling rocks

Q104/ This Traffic Sign Indicates That:

1- Hazardous material are not permitted on this road
2- A warning of hazardous montains
3- No vehicles on train track

Q105/ This Traffic Sign Indicates That:

1- This is a tow away zone
2- A construction zone
3- Machiney on road be cautious

Q106/ This Traffic Sign Indicates That:

1- Watch for people crossing your path
2- No passing zone
3- Work zone ahead

Q107/ This Traffic Sign Indicates That you are coming to a:

1- School zone
2- Playground
3- Residential area

Q108/ This Traffic Sign Indicates That:

1- Snowmobiles parking
2- Snowmobiles may use this road
3- Snowmobiles cannot use this road

Q109/ This Traffic Sign Indicates That:

1- 4-way lanes in the highway ahead
2- 4-way stop sign in the intersection ahead
3- This sign is for 4 way lanes roadways, generally found in big cities.

Q110/ This Traffic Sign Indicates That:

1- A construction zone is ahead
2- A bridge or viaduct is ahead
3- Bumpy or uneven road is ahead

Q111/ Does This Traffic Sign Indicates That :

1- A school bus stop is ahead. Watch for kids and school buses with flashing red lights
2- A school zone is ahead
3- A University campus is ahead, watch out for juveniles and upcoming traffic when the stoplight is red

Q112/ This Traffic Sign Indicates That:

1- Parking is by permit only
2- Person with special needs transport
3- This parking space is reserved exclusively for vehicles that display a valid Accessible Parking Permit

Q113/ This Traffic Sign Indicates That:

1- An intersection ahead
2- Added lane on the right right
3- an upcoming curve on the right

Q114/ This Traffic Sign Indicates That:

1- An incident on the road
2- Unpaved roadway ahead
3- The road has no outlet or continuation

Q115/ This Traffic Sign Indicates That:

1- Highway exit
2- Intersection exit
3- Detour marking change in direction

Q116/ This Traffic Sign Indicates That:

1- Rest area in one mile
2- Rest area in one kilometer
3- None of the above

Q117/ What does this road sign mean?

1- The road shoulder is much lower than the road surface.
2- There is gravel on the road.
3- The road is slippery and wet

Q118/ This Traffic Sign Indicates That:

1- There is roadwork ahead
2- You must change lanes ahead
3- There is a detour ahead

Q119/ This Traffic Sign Indicates That:

1- Slight bend ahead
2- Sharp bend ahead
3- Special lane entry

Q120/ This Traffic Sign Indicates That:

1- May turn left only on a green arrow
2- May turn left on a green light when it is safe
3- Must wait for the solid green light before you turn left

Q121/ This Traffic Sign Indicates That:

1- No left turns are allowed
2- A right turn is ahead
3- A hidden intersection ahead that may cause an obstructed view

Q122/ This Traffic Sign Indicates That:

1- The speed limit under adverse weather condition should be between 30-55 mph
2- The minimum speed limit is 30 mph
3- The maximum speed limit is 30 mph

Q123/ This Traffic Sign Indicates That:

1- No turns on red stoplight
2- turn only if the intersection is clear
3- No left turn only in the intersection ahead

Q124/ What does this road sign mean?

1- Prepare to stop
2- A rest area to the right
3- Change in direction displayed via the arrow

Q125/ If you see a flag person on the road, it means that

1- you must increase your speed.
2- you must go straight.
3- you must obey the flag person's instructions.

Q126/ What does this road sign mean?

1- A divided highway ends
2- A dead end, traffic can only proceed by turning to the left or right direction
3- You are entering a 4 legged intersection with a divided highway

Q127/ A pennant-shaped sign indicates

1- you must keep right
2- a no-passing zone
3- an emergency stop

Q128/ What does this road sign mean?

1- A railroad crossing ahead
2- A one-way road ahead
3- A narrow bridge ahead

Q129/ What does this road sign mean?

1- There is a detour ahead
2- There is a low place in the road ahead
3- There is a bump in the road ahead

Q130/ This Traffic Sign Indicates That:

1- Small trucks only
2- No Truck of 10 feet in height
3- No trucks are allowed in this lane

Q131/ The motorist on the vehicle ahead signals that

1- He intend to make a left turn
2- He is slowing down or stopping
3- You have his permission to pass

Q132/ This Traffic Sign Indicates That:

1- No right turn at all time
2- No right turn only when the traffic light is red
3- You can only go straight

Q133/ What does this road sign mean?

1- Railroad crossing ahead
2- You will enconter a railway crossing when turning right
3- You will enconter a railway crossing when turning left

Q134/ Does This Traffic Sign Indicates That :

1- Sharp right turn ahead
2- A road joins from the right
3- The road ahead turns sharply right then sharply left

Q136/ This Traffic Sign Indicates That:

1- Karaoke
2- Call center
3- Phone station

Q135/ This Traffic Sign Indicates That:

1- You should not enter between the times and dates mentioned
2- No buses are authorized
3- This lane is exclusively reserved for a certain type of vehicle and during certain days and time

Q138/ This Traffic Sign Indicates That:

1- A sharp bend left turn a cross road
2- A curve left with a Cross Road
3- No left turn in the intersection ahead

Q137/ This Traffic Sign Indicates That:

1- Y- intersection
2- V- intersection
3- T- intersection

Q140/ This Traffic Sign Indicates That:

1- Destination sign indicating the direction to two cities
2- A reminder of the distance left to both cities
3- An interstate route

Q139/ This Traffic Sign Indicates That:

1- Divided highway with light rail transit crossing
2- Don't cross the train track, go right or left
3- None of the above

Q141/ Does This Traffic Sign Indicate:

1- This is a temporarily closed lane. You should reduce your speed and follow the direction indicated by the arrow
2- An arrow that shows highway entry
3- Temporary work on this route, please exit

Q142/ The motorist on the vehicle ahead signals that

1-He intend to make a right turn
2-He is slowing down or stopping
3-You have his permission to pass

Q143/ This Traffic Sign Indicates That:

1- 500 feet until destination
2- A supplementary sign that adds more information regarding the distance
3- A tall vehicle warning

Q144/ This Traffic Sign Indicates That:

1- US route marker
2- Interstate highway sign
3- Services and shops 40 miles ahead

Q145/ This Traffic Sign Indicates That:

1- Side Road on the right
2- A curve on the right
3- A sharp bend on the right

Q146/ This Traffic Sign Indicates That:

1- A light rail is proceeding, do not stop
2- Low ground clearance
3- No commercial vehicle allowed to cross the track

Q147/ This Traffic Sign Indicates That:

1- Do not pass until you pass the sign
2- Do not pass unless it seems safe to do so
3- Do not pass for any reason

Q148/ This Traffic Sign Indicates That:

1- Seat belts are required for your safety
2- Pedestrians aren't allowed
3- Bus company on the right

Q149/ This Traffic Sign Indicates That:

1- Rail Transit Station
2- Railway crossing
3- Divided highway with light rail transit crossing

Q150/ This Traffic Sign Indicates That:

1- Curve and the advisory speed
2- Curve in 35 feet
3- an angle of 35 degree on this curve

PART 1
ANSWERS :

Q1/ The answer is 2- U-Turn is not allowed

Q2/ The answer is 2- You are entering a school zone

Q3/ The answer is 3- A hospital

Q4/ The answer is 2- Do not stand or stop in this area

Q5/ The answer is 3- Deer can cross

Q6/ The answer is 2- You need to keep right of the obstacle (median, traffic island, etc.)

Q7/ The answer is 3- Railroad crossing

Q8/ The answer is 1-regulatory sign

Q9/ The answer is 1- Workers on the road ahead symbol

Q10/ The answer is 1- Drive to the right

Q11/ The answer is 2- A lane usage road sign authorizing right turn only

Q12/ The answer is 3- A stoplight is ahead

Q13/ The answer is 2- No bicycles are allowed on this road

Q14/ The answer is 3- You should stop and yield the right-of-way to passing vehicles from both directions

Q15/ The answer is 2- You will share the road with oncoming traffic

Q16/ The answer is 1- An intersection is ahead

Q17/ The answer is 1- Airport

Q18/ The answer is 2- Us numbered route sign

Q19/ The answer is 1- Alert slow-moving vehicle

Q20/ The answer is 1- Pavement is grooved

Q21/ The answer is 3- Driving straight through the intersection isn't permitted

Q22/ The answer is 1- The road ahead is separated by a median; keep to the right, in other words a divided highway begins

Q23/ The answer is 1- Passing isn't allowed in this area

Q24/ The answer is 2- An upcoming roundabout and information about directions

Q25/ The answer is 3- Two way left turn lane

Q26/ The answer is 3- No vehicles on train track

Q27/ The answer is 2- A pedestrian crosswalk

Q28/ The answer is 1- Electric charging vehicle station

Q29/ The answer is 3- Lane merging from the right side, vehicles coming from both roads are equally responsible to merge correctly

Q30/ The answer is 1- No Littering is allowed

Q31/ The answer is 2- A right lane end is ahead; in case you drive In the right lane, you need to merge with traffic into the left

Q32/ The answer is 3- Drawbridge ahead (*Bridge that lifts or swings to allow boats to pass*)

Q33/ The answer is 2- Do not enter this road

Q34/ The answer is 1- The ending of a high occupancy vehicle lane

Q35/ The answer is 2- Traffic may only travel in one direction

Q36/ The answer is 1- You may not park between the signs during the posted time

Q37/ The answer is 2- A winding road is ahead

Q38/ The answer is 3- A maximum speed limit is determined on the curve

Q39/ The answer is 2- Disabeled person parking

Q40/ The answer is 3- Slower traffic you need to keep or move to the right

Q41/ The answer is 3- Underpass, be cautious if your vehicle is over 12.6"

Q42/ The answer is 3- Speed limit will change to a maximum speed of 50MPH

Q43/ The answer is 1- No right turns on red

Q44/ The answer is 2- A divided highway ends

Q45/ The answer is 3- There may be water flowing over the road

Q46/ The answer is 2- A hazard sign, the downward line reveals the side on which you can safely pass

Q47/ The answer is 1 - A permissive sign

Q48/ The answer is 2- A roundabout is ahead

Q49/ The answer is 3- Two or more passengers in the vehicle are required to take the left lane

Q50/ The answer is 2- You are coming to a bus station

Q51/ The answer is 2- During school hours and when the yellow lights are flashing obey this speed limits

Q52/ The answer is 1- You should not stop in the space between the signs

Q53/ The answer is 2- There is a sharp bend or turn ahead

Q54/ The answer is 2- A sideroad

Q55/ The answer is 2- Passing is strictly not allowed

Q56/ The answer is 3- Steep hill

Q57/ The answer is 3- Pharmacy

Q58/ The answer is 3- A person who controls the traffic is ahead

Q59/ The answer is 1- A railroad crossing is ahead

Q60/ The answer is 2- The maximum speed limit at night

Q61/ The answer is 3- A stop sign is ahead

Q62/ The answer is 3- Slow down, stop if necessary, and yield

Q63/ The answer is 1- You are not allowed to go straight, only left or right turns

Q64/ The answer is 2- This is a guide for drivers in order to warn you of a change in direction

Q65/ The answer is 2- A Survey crew working

Q66/ The answer is 1- A risk of falling rocks

Q67/ The answer is 2- Road becomes slippery when wet

Q68/ The answer is 1- Allow space between your vehicle and cyclists

Q69/ The answer is 1- Road forks to the right

Q70/ The answer is 3- Interchange direction sign

Q71/ The answer is 3- The left lane ahead is closed due to roadwork. respect the speed limitation

Q72/ The answer is 1- Bicycle crossing ahead or bicycle usually use this road

Q73/ The answer is 3- A railroad crossing is ahead

Q74/ The answer is 1- Heavy trucks are allowed

Q75/ The answer is 2- A route to avoid a construction zone or even a severe traffic collision

Q76/ The answer is 1- An interstate highway marker

Q77/ The answer is 1- A Light rail is activated

Q78/ The answer is 1- A T-intersection ahead, you can only turn right or left

Q79/ The answer is 1- Pedestrians aren't permitted

Q80/ The answer is 3- Road curves right then left

Q81/ The answer is 2- Narrow road ahead

Q82/ The answer is 2- Left turn is not allowed at the junction ahead

Q83/ The answer is 1- Facilities accessible for disabled persons

Q84/ The answer is 3- When flashing, you are advised to keep to the right and drive responsibly

Q85/ The answer is 2- The road ahead sharply turn left then right

Q86/ The answer is 1- You are allowed to park in this space

Q87/ The answer is 3- No hitchhiking

Q88/ The answer is 3- A warning sign

Q89/ The answer is 2- temporary Speed Limit on a construction area

Q90/ The answer is 1- A temporary winding road

Q91/ The answer is 2- Flashing lights showing the direction

Q92/ The answer is 3- All answers above are correct

Q93/ The answer is 2- A network of highway across our country

Q94/ The answer is 3- Traffic may pass the obstruction on left or right

Q95/ The answer is 3- Special vehicles may take this lane either at all times or during certain hours

Q96/ The answer is 2- Do not turn left during the times shown bellow

Q97/ The answer is 3- The direction you must follow at a roundabout

Q98/ The answer is 1- Never drive past this sign

Q99/ The answer is 1- Offset side roads are ahead

Q100/ The answer is 2- Emergency Medical Services

Q101/ The answer is 2- You are allowed to park only for 1 hour

Q102/ The answer is 2- When turning yield to pedestrians

Q103/ The answer is 1- A paved surface ends ahead

Q104/ The answer is 1- Hazardous material are not permitted on this road

Q105/ The answer is 1- This is a tow away zone

Q106/ The answer is 3- Work zone

Q107/ The answer is 2 Playground

Q108/ The answer is 2- Snowmobiles may use this road

Q109/ The answer is 2- 4-way stop sign in the junction ahead

Q110/ The answer is 3- Bumpy or uneven road is ahead

Q111/ The answer is 1-Watch for kids and school buses with flashing red lights

Q112/ The answer is 3- Parking for vehicles with accessible Parking Permit

Q113/ The answer is 2- Added lane on the right right

Q114/ The answer is 3- The road has no outlet or continuation

Q115/ The answer is 1- Highway exit

Q116/ The answer is 1- Rest area in one mile

Q117/ The answer is 1-The shoulder is much lower than the surface.

Q118/ The answer is 1- There is roadwork ahead

Q119/ The answer is 1- Slight bend

Q120/ The answer is 2- May turn left on a green light when it is safe

Q121/ The answer is 3- A hidden intersection ahead

Q122/ The answer is 2- The minimum speed limit is 30 mph

Q123/ The answer is 1- No turns on red stoplight

Q124/ The answer is 3- Change in direction displayed via the arrow

Q125/ The answer is 3- you must obey the flag person's instructions.

Q126/ The answer is 3- You are entering a 4 legged intersection with a divided highway

Q127/ The answer is 2- a no-passing zone.

Q128/ The answer is 1- A narrow bridge ahead

Q129/ The answer is 2- Low place

Q130/ The answer is 3- No trucks are allowed in this lane

Q131/ The answer is 1- He intend to make a left turn

Q132/ The answer is 2- No right turn on red

Q133/ The answer is 3- *A* railway crossing on the left road

Q134/ The answer is 3- The road ahead turns sharply right then left

Q135 / The answer is 3- This lane is reserved for a certain type of vehicle and during certain days and time

Q136/The answer is 3- Phonestation

Q137/ The answer is 2- Y-intersection

Q138/ The answer is 2- A **c**urve left with a Cross Road

Q139/ The answer is 1- Divided highway with light rail crossing

Q140/ The answer is 1- Destination sign indicating the direction to two cities

Q141/ The answer is 1- This is a temporarily closed lane. follow the direction indicated by the arrow

Q142/ The answer is 1- He intend to make a right turn

Q143/ The answer is 2- A supplementary sign that adds more information regarding the distance

Q144/ The answer is 1- US route marker

Q145/ The answer is 1- Side Road on the right

Q146/ The answer is 2- Low ground clearance

Q147/ The answer is 3- Do not pass

Q148/ The answer is 1- Seat belts are required for your safety

Q149/ The answer is 1- Rail Transit Station

Q150/ The answer is 1- Curve and the advisory speed

7

<u>Section 2</u>
Rules of The Road

Q01/ When driving at the posted speed limit during nighttime, what factor increases the risk compared to daytime driving?

A. At night, your reaction time is four times slower
B. At night, your braking time is four-time slower
C. At night, you cannot see very far ahead
D. Some drivers have made it illegal to drive with just their parking lights on

Q02/You are considered legally intoxicated in the state of North Carolina if your blood alcohol level (BAC) is

_____ or above.

A. 0.5
B. 0.05
C. 0.8
D. 0.08

Q03/ On multilane roads, if your intention is to drive slower than the flow of traffic, in which lane you should drive

A. The middle lane
B. The rightmost lane
C. The leftmost lane
D. You can drive in any lane if you respect the posted speed limits

Q04/ Who has the right of way at a roundabout

A. Vehicles who prepare to exit the roundabout
B. Large vehicles over small vehicles as they have wide blind spots
C. Vehicles on the right
D. Traffic already at the roundabout

Q05/ Which device from the following is illegal to use while driving

A. A mobile phone
B. A computer
C. A tablet
D. A, B and C are all correct, hence D is the right answer

Q06/ What distinguishes a controlled intersection from an uncontrolled intersection?

A. Controlled intersections are typically wider and found in metropolitan areas
B. Uncontrolled intersections always have police officers for traffic control
C. Controlled intersections are managed by traffic control signs and signals
D. Controlled intersections are managed by police officers

Q07/ Reducing speed solely to observe accidents or any unusual occurrences.

A. Can prevent rear-end accidents
B. Can lead to a better traffic flow
C. Demonstrates defensive driving behavior
D. Will lead to traffic congestion

Q08/ What is the purpose of using your vehicle's signals while turning?

A. To communicate your intentions to other vehicles in traffic.
B. To alert pedestrians to your presence
C. To facilitate a smoother traffic flow
D. A, B and C are all correct, hence D is the right answer

Q09/ What are the tell-tale signs that the pedestrian crossing the intersection is blind

A. They often wear an orange hat and a black sunglass
B. They are often guided by a family member or a friend hence they can be easily identifiable
C. The usage of guide dogs and orange canes
D. The usage of guide dogs and white canes

Q10/ What does a red curb indicate

A. No passing is allowed
B. Stopping is allowed
C. No Parking is allowed in this area
D. Parking is allowed in this area

Q11/ In which situations can you execute a left turn on a red light?

A. Only from a two-way street onto another two-way street
B. Only when the intersection is blocked
C. Only from a one-way street onto another one-way street
D. At your own discretion regardless of the street type

Q12/ A solid yellow line marked on the pavement indicates that

A. The road that you travel on is a one-way road
B. The road that you travel on allows you to travel in one direction only
C. You can't cross this line to pass or turn
D. You can cross this line to pass or turn

Q13/ Shoulder checks are an essential defensive driving skill because

A. They communicate your intentions of changing lanes and help you determine who is driving behind you
B. They are crucial to alert oncoming vehicles of hazards or emergency situations
C. They will assist you while changing lanes, as regardless of your mirror's adjustment, there will always be a blind spot
D. A, B and C are all correct, hence D is the right answer

Q14/ What is the role of a shared center lane

A. Reserved for vehicles that have a special permit
B. Parking or stopping
C. Making a right turn onto a major thoroughfare
D. Making two-way left turns

Q15/ What is the timeframe within which you should inform the DMV about changing your address or updating your name?

A. 10 days
B. 30 days
C. 60 days
D. 90 days

Q16/ By law you are required to follow the instructions from

A. A security guard at a residential area
B. A parent at a school zone
C. A flagger or a flagman
D. A, B & C are all correct, hence D is the right answer

Q17/ When a police officer signals you to pull over, what is your legal obligation?

A. Immediately stop your vehicle in the current lane of travel
B. Gradually and safely come to a full stop by moving to the right side of the road
C. Politely decline the officer's request and accelerate your vehicle.
D. If you have a legitimate reason, ensure a complete stop of your vehicle

Q18/ The first rule of a safe and legal turn is

A. to increase your speed
B. to reduce your speed
C. to cut corners while turning
D. to move into the proper lane well before the turn

Q19/ What is the best course of action if you miss your exit on an interstate highway?

A. Continue to the next exit.
B. Stop and ask for help.
C. Back up to reach your exit.
D. Make a U-turn to reach your exit

Q20/ At an intersection where a pedestrian is crossing and the traffic lights switch from red to green, what should you do

A. Yield to the pedestrian and allow them to complete their crossing.
B. Safely proceed as you have the right of way.
C. Use your horn to alert the pedestrian to give you the way.
D. Blame the pedestrian for crossing slowly

Q21/If your driver's license is suspended due to the point system in North Carolina, how long may it be taken away for the first suspension?

A. 30 days
B. 45 days
C. 60 days
D. 90 days

Q22/ When you find yourself in an intersection and hear the siren of an emergency vehicle, what should you do?

A. Move to the right and stop at the intersection
B. Continue through the intersection, then pull over to the left and stop
C. Move to the left and stop at the intersection
D. Continue through the intersection, then pull over to the right and stop

Q23/ What factors can influence your blood alcohol content?

A. The amount of alcohol you've consumed
B. Your fitness level
C. The type of alcohol you've been drinking
D. Your height

Q24/ If your parked car unintentionally rolls and collides with another unattended vehicle, what should you do?

A. Activate your horn to alert others to the situation
B. Move your car and carry on with your journey
C. Notify the police about the incident

Q25/ If you are at a red light and the intersection is blocked, what is the appropriate action to take when the light turns green?

A. Proceed cautiously, ensuring your chances of clearing the intersection are high
B. Stop until the intersection is no longer blocked by traffic, then proceed
C. Sound your horn to encourage other vehicles to move quickly
D. Make a U-turn and change your roadway, helping to clear the blocked intersection

Q26/ During adverse weather conditions such as fog rain or snow you are required to

A. Use your emergency flashers for better vision
B. Use your low-beam headlights for better vision
C. Use your parking lights for better vision
D. Use your horns to communicate your intentions

Q27/ Who has the right-of-way first at an uncontrolled intersection

A. Vehicles on the right
B. Vehicles on the left
C. The vehicle that arrives first
D. Vehicles going straight

Q28/ What is the cause of skidding?

A. Slippery roads
B. Acceleration
C. Outdated tires
D. A, B & C are all correct, hence D is the right answer

Q29/ You are driving and you encounter an intersection where the stoplight is red, but you have instructions from a police officer signaling you to proceed

A. Obey the officer's instructions by proceeding
B. Stop to see what other drivers doing before making a decision
C. Wait for the stoplight switch to green
D. Alert the officer that he is not paying attention to the color of the light

Q30/ What is the minimum amount of liability insurance required for covering all personal injuries in a crash in North Carolina?

A. $30,000
B. $45,000
C. $50,000
D. $60,000

Q31/ At night, you should dim your headlights to low beam whenever you are

A. within 300 feet of a vehicle you are following.
B. within 500 feet of an oncoming vehicle.
C. driving on a well-lit road
D. in all of the above situations.

Q32/ Which option from the following is a sign of hydroplaning?

A. Increase in fuel consumption
B. Low visibility due to fog
C. Degradation of steering and braking control
D. A misfiring engine

Q33/ When going down a steep hill while driving a manual transmission what should you do

A. turn on your emergency flashers
B. keep applying your brakes
C. shift into a higher gear
D. shift into a lower gear

Q34/ In North Carolina, Traffic at roundabouts travels in a counterclockwise direction

A. False, it depends on the state or province laws and regulations
B. This statement is true
C. False, in North America, the traffic at a roundabout travels in a clockwise direction
D. False, it depends on the instructions that the road signs convey before entering the roundabout

Q35/ What is the best driving strategy during adverse weather resulting in a slippery road

A. Reduce your following distance
B. Increase your following distance
C. Make sure to repetitively use your ABS
D. All of the answers above

Q36/ An individual whose driver's privilege is suspended/revoked may

A. Operate their car in certain emergency situations.
B. Under no circumstances operate a motor vehicle.
C. Drive to and from their workplace if they can provide a justification.
D. Operate a vehicle with the assistance of another fully licensed driver.

Q37/ The crucial aspect to bear in mind when it comes to managing speed on curved roads is

A. Maintain the posted speed limit as you approach the curve, then reduce speed at the sharpest part
B. Decelerate before entering the curve
C. Gradually increase speed before entering the curve

Q38/ Unbalanced tires are due to which problem from the following?

A. Weak shock absorbers
B. Not having enough fuel
C. Using the ABS excessively
D. Uneven distribution of weight around the tire

Q39/ While driving you notice a slow-moving vehicle ahead. What is the best action to take before overtaking it?

A. Ensure good visibility, use your turn signal or horn, and check for any passing prohibition signs
B. Make sure the pavement line is solid yellow
C. Only overtake when approaching a bend or curve
D. Tailgate and sound your horn before passing

Q40 / Prior to making a left turn from a one-way street, where should your vehicle be positioned

A. As far left as possible
B. As far right as possible
C. Regardless of the lane
D. To the far right

Q41/ What is the best precautionary action to take if you are blinded by an oncoming vehicle's high-beam lights while driving at night?

A. Change your lane immediately
B. Sound your horns and alert the driver
C. Use your high beam as well so he will understand that he is causing discomfort to other drivers
D. Look at the right side of the road

Q42/What variable from the following can make your reaction time prolonged

A. An exhaustion
B. Some medications
C. Driving under the influence of alcohol or drugs
D. A, B & C are all correct, therefore D is the right answer

Q43/ There are two lines in the center of the road dividing traffic. One is a solid line while the other is a broken one. the line on your side is solid

A. This line divides traffic traveling in opposite directions
B. It is safe to pass and overtake
C. Passing is not allowed
D. You can only make a U-turn

Q44/ What is a detour and what purpose it serve?

A. A high occupancy vehicle lane or road
B. An interstate/province highway
C. A high-speed tollway
D. A temporary alternative roadway to avoid congestion or bypass a closed road

Q45/ Flashing yellow lights indicate that you should

A. Treat the intersection as a stop sign intersection, meaning you should stop and give the right-of-way
B. Proceed without stopping as you have the right to do so
C. Treat the intersection as a yield sign, meaning you should slow down and stop if necessary and give the right-of-way
D. Stop and wait for the light to turn green before proceeding

Q46/ According to North Carolina insurance law, what is the minimum injury liability coverage for one person in an accident?

A. $10,000
B. $20,000
C. $30,000
D. $40,000

Q47/ When turning left at an intersection, it is important to give priority to:

A. Traffic behind you
B. Traffic on the right side
C. Traffic coming from the opposite direction
D. You don't have to yield to anyone

Q48/ When the posted speed limit on a road is 55mph and the road is wet, what should you do?

A. Drive 5 to 10 MPH under the speed limit
B. Maintain a speed of 55 MPH
C. Drive 20 to 25 MPH under the speed limit
D. Test your brakes frequently

Q49/ You are approaching an intersection where traffic lights are not functioning. How should you handle this situation?

A. Yield to traffic from your left side only before proceeding
B. Yield to traffic from your right side only before proceeding
C. If traffic signals are not working, it means there is no reason for traffic control, so you have the right of way at all times.
D. Treat this situation as if you are entering an all-way stop sign junction

Q50/ To maintain alertness and prevent highway hypnosis during extended expressway journeys, what should you do?

A. Engage in eye exercises.
B. Send text messages.
C. Have phone conversations.
D. Consume stimulants

Q51/What type of seatbelt system should be used for children under 8 years old and weighing less than 80 pounds?

A. The same seatbelt system as for adults
B. A lap and shoulder seatbelt system
C. Weight-appropriate child passenger restraint system
D. No seatbelt is required for children under 8

Q52/ You may lend your issued driver's license to another driver

A. If he has an immediate emergence
B. If his driving privilege is suspended
C. If you are confident of his driving skills
D. Under no circumstances

Q53/ What should you do if you and another vehicle arrive at an uncontrolled intersection at the same time?

A. It's up to you to choose who goes first because there is no specific right-of-way law in this situation.
B. The vehicle on the right has the right of way in this scenario.
C. The vehicle on the left has the right of way in this scenario.
D. The vehicle with the loudest horn

Q54/ What is the first thing to do if you are the first person to come upon the scene of a collision

A. Move injured bodies off the road
B. Call the local authorities and ask for an ambulance if needed
C. exchange insurance information
D. Call the injured person's family or friends

Q55/ What is a true characteristic of roadways on bridges and overpasses during cold, wet weather?

A. They have a tendency to freeze earlier than the rest of the road
B. They do not freeze because they are constructed from concrete.
C. They tend to freeze at the same time as the rest of the road.
D. They usually freeze after the rest of the road does.

Q56/ What is the term for the minimum following distance or time used to drive safely in normal weather conditions?

A. The one second rule
B. The two second rule
C. The three second rule
D. The four second rule

Q57/ When entering a highway from an acceleration lane, what are you required to do as you merge into traffic

A. Stop and then proceed
B. Slow down and then proceed
C. Yield the right of way to traffic already on the highway
D. Only yield if there is a yield sign indicating this instruction

Q58/ In North Carolina, what is the statutory speed limit in school zone area

A. 10 MPH
B. 15 MPH
C. 20 MPH
D. 25 MPH

Q59/ Your braking distance can be increased on construction sites

A. If there is no pavement marking to assist drivers
B. If there are no flaggers to assist drivers
C. Because there may be oil used on construction sites that can make your braking prolonged
D. Because construction sites have people working in them

Q60/ What is the requirement for a permit holder while operating a motor vehicle on highways?

A. They must operate the vehicle alone
B. They must have a licensed person accompany them and sit beside them in the vehicle
C. They should be accompanied by any licensed person in the vehicle
D. They are not allowed to drive on highways

Q61/ When driving behind a large truck on the freeway, what is the recommended approach?

A. Maintain a closer following distance compared to a passenger vehicle
B. Keep a greater following distance than you would for a passenger vehicle
C. Pass the truck promptly on its left side
D. Pass the truck swiftly on its right side

Q62/ What is the correct hand signal to indicate a left turn when driving a vehicle?

A. Hand and arm extended outward
B. Hand and arm extended upward
C. Hand and arm extended downward
D. Hand and arm extended backward

Q63/ Parking in a disabled person parking area is

A. Allowed if you can get back quickly
B. Only allowed if you have a disabled parking permit
C. Allowed at all times
D. Allowed only during low traffic hours

Q64/ What is the best measure to prevent hydroplaning?

A. Reduce your speed on adverse weather conditions.
B. Make sure that your vehicle's tires have good tread depth.
C. Make sure that your vehicle's tires are properly inflated with the required tire pressure.
D. A, B, and C are all correct, thus D is the right answer

Q65/What should you do when you park your vehicle facing uphill next to a curb?

A. Set the hand brake and keep the wheels straight
B. Set the hand brake and turn the wheels toward the curb
C. Set the hand brake, also turn your wheels away from the curb
D. Put the transmission in first gear

Q66/ Flashing red lights indicate that you should

A. Treat the intersection as a stop sign intersection, meaning you should stop and give the right-of-way
B. Proceed without stopping as you have the right to do so
C. Treat the intersection as a yield sign
D. Stop and wait for the light to turn green before proceeding

Q67/ How much time does a new resident in North Carolina have to obtain a North Carolina driver's license or learner permit after establishing residence in the state?

A. 30 days
B. 45 days
C. 60 days
D. 90 days

Q68/ When should you use your vehicle's high-beam headlights?

A. In well-lit urban areas with streetlights.
B. When driving on unlit rural roads.
C. During heavy rain and fog.
D. When approaching oncoming traffic

Q69/ Which measure can help manage sun glare while driving?

A. Ensure your car visor is functional and free of obstructions
B. Keep the inside and outside of your windshield clean and wear polarized sunglasses
C. Both A and B are correct
D. Ignore the glare and continue driving

Q70/ While driving through an intersection, what message does a red light followed by a green arrow convey?

A. You are allowed to proceed in all directions except the one indicated by the arrow
B. This traffic control signal allows pedestrians to cross the intersection. Treat this situation as a yield sign
C. You are allowed to proceed in the direction the arrow indicates without stopping

Q71/ Unbalanced tires or low tire pressures can lead to

A. Faster tire wear.
B. Decreased stopping distance
C. Increased fuel economy
D. All of the above (A, B, and C) are correct, making D the right answer

Q72/ When should you perform a shoulder check?

A. After completing a maneuver
B. When roads are crowded and the traffic is chaotic
C. Before changing lanes, making a turn, or entering a roadway with a yield sign
D. Whenever your gut tells you to do so

Q73/ All jurisdictions in North America consider Tailgating as a/an

A. Smart driving skill that helps reduce congestion on our roadways
B. Great occasional skill that can be used to reduce congestion on our roadways
C. Immature and aggressive maneuvers that endanger road users and lead to collisions
D. Felony that leads to jail time

Q74/ Which statement from the following is a crucial parking rule?

A. Do not park on a Highway
B. Never park close to a fire hydrant
C. Never Park on a curve or bend
D. A, B & C are all correct, therefore D is the right answer

Q75/ If your chemical test reveals a blood alcohol concentration of 0.08% or higher, your driver's license will be suspended for a minimum of how many days?

A. 90
B. 30
C. 120
D. 60

Q76/ Parking close to a curve is prohibited because

A. You will need to pay the meter first
B. It is designated for loading shipments
C. It is reserved for disabled people parking
D. You will obstruct the visibility of other road users and increase hazards on the road

Q77/ To ensure safety while overtaking a motorcycle, you should take the following precautions:

A. Sound your horn before passing.
B. Leave a cautionary space as motorcycles are more vulnerable
C. Before you pass, turn on the high-beam lights.
D. Turn your emergency flashers to alert other drivers of your intention

Q78/ What is the maximum speed limit on North Carolina interstates?

A. Between 35 and 45 mph
B. A minimum of 70 mph
C. A maximum of 70 mph
D. Between 50 and 65 mph

Q79/ What is the initial step for safe and defensive passing on a multilane highway?

A. Slowing down
B. Check your rearview mirror.
C. Use your turn signals.
D. Use a hand signal to alert oncoming vehicles

Q80/ What is the requirement for a vehicle approaching a railroad crossing protected by flashing red lights?

A. Come to a full stop not less than five feet from the nearest track
B. Come to a full stop not less than ten feet from the nearest track
C. Come to a full stop not less than fifteen feet and not more than fifty feet from the nearest track
D. Slow down and proceed with caution without stopping

Q81/ One of the individuals involved in an accident is severely injured, What should you do as a protective measure

A. Move his body immediately off the road as he can't move
B. Protect the scene of the accident and call an ambulance for him
C. Call his family or friends to discuss the accident with them
D. Use their vehicle as a shield to protect the scene of the accident

Q82/ When there isn't sufficient space for a U-turn, what type of turn should you make?

A. A two-point turn.
B. A five-point turn.
C. A four-point turn.
D. A three-point turn.

Q83/ Changing lanes on a multi-lane roundabout is

A. Allowed at all times
B. Generally prohibited as it can be a very dangerous maneuver
C. It is allowed on multilane roundabouts and prohibited on single lane roundabouts
D. Allowed only if you have a fully graduated license or a commercial license as a sign of competency in performing such a high-risk maneuver

Q84/ If you come up on several snowplows clearing a freeway, you should not

A. Wait for the plows to allow traffic to safely pass
B. Try to pass between them
C. Keep a safe distance
D. Do any of the above

Q85/ What is the correct action to take when you approach a school bus stopped on an undivided roadway with its red lights flashing?

A. Come to a complete stop and wait until the red lights are turned off.
B. Maintain your current speed.
C. Reduce your speed and proceed cautiously.
D. Accelerate and pass the bus swiftly.

Q86/ When at the crest of a grade where your vehicle is not visible to oncoming traffic from the opposite direction, which action should you avoid?

A. Using your hands-free device
B. Proceeding straight forward
C. Making a U-turn
D. Making a right turn

Q87/ What is the recommended course of action if you receive a call while operating a vehicle?

A. Pullover and park before answering the call.
B. Answer the call immediately to find out what's happening.
C. Only answer the phone if you are anticipating an important call.
D. Text back and inform the caller that you are driving

Q88/ As per the North Carolina laws and regulations, the likelihood of getting into an accident rises when your blood alcohol concentration reaches which of the following levels?

A. 0.02%
B. 0.08%
C. 0.05%
D. 0.10%

Q89/ If your license is revoked/suspended due to your refusal to undergo chemical testing for drugs or alcohol, you might qualify for restricted driving privileges after a specific duration of the revocation period has passed. How long is this waiting period?

A. 4 months
B. 6 months
C. 12 months
D. 15 months

Q90/ Safely backing includes all the following measures expect

A. Looking over your rearview mirrors
B. Alerting traffic of your intentions
C. Checking behind your car before you get in
D. Tapping your horn before you back up

Q91/ How can you use your ABS

A. Use the handbrakes and steer in the left direction
B. Use the handbrakes and steer in the right direction
C. Maintain firm pressure on the brake while steering
D. Maintain gradual pressure on the brake while steering

Q92/ When vehicles are traveling at 60 mph and are faced with an abrupt need to stop, which vehicle will require the greatest stopping distance?

A. A passenger car
B. A van
C. A truck or commercial vehicle
D. A Bicycle

Q93/ Carbon monoxide is an odorless and colorless gas produced by engines. What are the early symptoms of carbon monoxide poisoning, and how should it be addressed?

A. Sudden fatigue, headache, and dizziness; the remedy is to get a good supply of fresh air
B. An increased excitation and alertness; the solution is to drive to your destination faster.
C. Sudden fatigue, headache, and dizziness; the treatment involves a cold application
D. A, B & C are all correct, hence D is the right answer

Q94/ What color is used to separate traffic traveling in the same direction

A. White lane marking
B. Grey lane marking
C. Yellow lane marking
D. Red lane marking

Q95/ According to North Carolina law, in cities and towns, what is the default speed limit unless otherwise posted?

A. 25 mph
B. 30 mph
C. 35 mph
D. 40 mph

Q96/ A lane marked with a diamond symbol is

A. an exit ramp.
B. a high-occupancy vehicle (HOV) lane or a restricted usage lane for buses and cabs/taxis
C. a turn lane.
D. an emergency-vehicle lane

Q97/ When to switch on the vehicle's headlights?

A. There is no specific time.
B. Between half an hour of sunset and half an hour of sunrise, and at any other time when visibility is low
C. Between 2 hours after sunset and 2 hours before sunrise
D. During rain or fog and adverse weather conditions

Q98/ What should you do if the light turns red while you are waiting to make a left turn at a junction?

A. Make your left turn in a safe manner
B. You are allowed to block the intersection in this specific case
C. Come to a complete stop before the intersection
D. Continue straight ahead or go back into the left turn lane by reversing

Q99 / If you hold a Limited Learner Permit, who is allowed to be in the front seat?

A. Only the driver
B. Only the supervising driver
C. The supervising driver, and passengers
D. No one except the driver and the supervising driver

Q100/ Why it's crucial to check for motorcycles before changing lanes?

A. Motorcycles are often difficult to spot due to their compact size.
B. Motorcycles are typically granted priority at intersections
C. Motorcycles are known for excessive speed.
D. Sharing traffic lanes with motorcycles is prohibited by law

Q101/ At night, if you need to stop immediately on a highway due to force majeure, what is legally required of you?

A. Stop immediately and turn on your high beams to alert oncoming traffic
B. Stop immediately and turn on your emergency flashers to alert oncoming traffic
C. Turn on your emergency flashers and if it is possible pull over to the edge of the road
D. Sound your horns actively to alert drivers around

Q102/ What is the minimum amount of liability insurance required for property damage in a crash in North Carolina?

A. $10,000
B. $50,000
C. $25,000
D. $15,000

Q103/ Is passing on the right legal in North Carolina?

A. No, it's always illegal
B. Yes, it's legal in all situations.
C. Yes, but only under specific conditions
D. Yes, it's legal as long as you honk your horn

Q104/ In a situation where 2 vehicles cross paths on a steep mountain, who is granted the right of way?

A. The ascending vehicle
B. Both vehicles
C. The descending vehicle
D. They should wait for a law enforcement officer to facilitate the passage of both vehicles

Q105/ How does marijuana affect a driver's ability to respond to sights and sounds?

A. It enhances their ability to respond to sights and sounds
B. It does no effect on their responsiveness
C. It makes it more difficult for them to respond to sights and sounds, lowering their ability to handle a quick series of tasks
D. It only affects their response to expected events

Q106/ Under which circumstances must you refrain from passing?

A. When approaching a school bus displaying flashing red lights and an extended stop arm.
B. When your lane is adjacent to a solid yellow line.
C. When encountering an upcoming hill or curve with limited visibility.
D. A, B, and C are all correct, hence D is the right answer

Q107/ Rear-end collisions frequently occur on highways due to

A. Driving under the influence of alcohol
B. Inadequate following distance
C. Neglecting to use headlights
D. Delayed braking response

Q108/ In areas with playing children while driving, expect:

A. Their awareness of safe crossing
B. Stopping at the curb before crossing
C. Potential sudden, inattentive running in front of your vehicle
D. Crossing only when with an adult

Q109/ If you experience a sudden flat tire while driving, What is your course of action?

A. Accelerate to gain control of your automobile
B. Firmly grip the steering wheel and keep the vehicle moving straight
C. Shift to the left side of the road
D. Apply the brakes to stop on the road

Q110/ What is the meaning of a red arrow signal at a junction?

A. You can turn in the arrow's direction
B. You must stop and wait for pedestrians to cross
C. Do not turn in the direction of the arrow and wait for a green signal or arrow
D. You can proceed with caution without waiting for a signal change

Q111/ What information from the following isn't important to exchange prior to a collision?

A. Making sure both parties agree about who is at fault
B. Full name and contact information of parties involved
C. Insurance policy information
D. Driver's license information

Q112/ What is the minimum duration of license revocation if you are convicted of driving more than 15 miles per hour over the speed limit, and your speed exceeds 55 mph?

A. 10 days
B. 15 days
C. 30 days
D. 60 days

SECTION 2: RULES OF THE ROAD

Q113/ On a two-lane, two-way road, a _____ allows you to cross over into the opposing lane temporarily to pass a vehicle if it is safe to do so.

A. Left arrow
B. Solid white line
C. Broken yellow line
D. Solid yellow line

Q114/ What should you do if your vehicle has stalled on railroad tracks, and you know that a train is approaching?

A. Quickly and safely get yourself and all passengers out of your vehicle and move as far away from the tracks as possible.
B. Roll down your window and open your doors to signal for help.
C. Keep trying to start the engine, and once it's running, drive your vehicle off the tracks.
D. Shift into neutral and attempt to push the vehicle off the tracks.

Q115/ What precautions should you take before opening the door of your parked vehicle on a roadside?

A. Ensure your phone is charged
B. Make sure your vehicle is in gear
C. Confirm that you will not endanger any person, vehicle, or traffic
D. Apply the parking brake

Q116/ If you are entering a roadway from a driveway or alley you must

A. Use your horns to alert traffic
B. Speed up to merge with existing traffic
C. Yield to vehicles already on the road
D. Only yield for pedestrians

Q117/ What is the primary role of flaggers on construction sites

A. To Administer DWI breath or urine tests for suspected drivers under the influence of alcohol
B. To clean roadways from oil that can lead to slippery condition
C. To alert and manage traffic entering a construction area by giving them directions to an exit or a detour
D. They have the same role and duties as law enforcement officers

Q118/ If your driver's license is revoked due to your refusal to undergo chemical testing for drugs or alcohol, the DMV will extend your license revocation for an additional period of:

A. 6 months
B. 30 days
C. 90 days
D. 12 months

Q119/ In North Carolina, when are you required to report a motor vehicle crash?

A. Only if someone is killed
B. Only if someone is hurt
C. If it causes $1,000 or more in property damage
D. None of the above

Q120/ Construction areas are generally marked by

A. Blue signs, flashy lights and pylons
B. Green signs, flashy lights and pylons
C. Red signs, flaggers, flashy lights and pylons
D. Orange signs, flaggers, flashy lights and pylons

Q121/ When driving in slow, heavy traffic and approaching a railroad track before an upcoming intersection, what should you do?

A. Wait until you can completely clear the railroad tracks before continuing
B. Stop just before the crossing gates in case they should close
C. Stop on the tracks until there is room in the intersection beyond them
D. Proceed cautiously, seeking an alternate route if possible

Q122/What is one of the mandatory insurance coverages that all drivers in North Carolina must carry?

A. Collision coverage
B. Comprehensive coverage
C. Liability insurance coverage
D. Rental car coverage

Q123/ Identify the cause of locked wheel skids

A. Not changing your tires on a regular basis or not following the user's guide recommended tire pressure
B. Pressing the gas and brake pedals simultaneously
C. Braking too hard at high speed
D. Shock absorbers failure to operate

Q124/ What is the maximum Blood alcohol content limit for individuals under the age of 21 in the state of North Carolina?

A. 0.04%
B. 0.08%
C. 0.00%
D. 0.10%

Q125/ What is the optimal choice a driver can make to recover from skidding?

A. Apply the brakes firmly.
B. Steer straight ahead.
C. Steer in the direction of the skid
D. Steer in the opposite direction of the skid

Q126/ If you and the driver on your left arrive at an intersection with stop signs on all four corners simultaneously, who has the right of way?

A. The driver on your left the right of way
B. You have the right of way
C. Whoever is courteous can give it
D. Whoever is signaling to make a turn has the right of way

Q127/ On multilane way roads, if your intention is to drive faster than the flow of traffic but never above the speed limit, in which lane you should drive

A. The middle lane
B. The rightmost lane
C. The leftmost lane
D. By law you can drive in any lane if you are respecting the posted speed limits

Q128/ Hands-free devices include

A. A cell phone fitted with an earpiece or headset capable of voice dialing.
B. A GPS device that is permanently mounted to the dashboard or another conveniently accessible position in the car.
C. Bluetooth earpiece
D. All of the proceedings

Q129/ What is the recommended seatbelt usage for all occupants in a vehicle, according to the information provided?

A. Lap belts only
B. No seatbelt is necessary with airbags
C. Both lap and shoulder belts on every trip
D. Shoulder belts only when traveling on highways

Q130 What are the three variables that constitute the stopping distance

A. The addition of the braking distance and reaction distance
B. The multiplication of the braking distance and reaction distance
C. The addition of the perception, reaction, and braking distance
D. The braking distance minus the reaction distance

Q131/ At a junction where a stop sign regulates traffic, if your line of sight to cross-street traffic is obstructed when you come to a stop behind the white bar marked on the road, what should you do?

A. Wait for 5 seconds, then continue
B. Honk your horn before moving forward
C. Lower your windows, listen for traffic, and then proceed.
D. Edge forward cautiously, check for both traffic and pedestrians, and proceed once it's safe

Q132/ Use your horn when

A. Another vehicle is in your way
B. It may help prevent a collision
C. A pedestrian is crossing slowly
D. Another driver makes a mistake

Q133/ The likelihood of Collision tends to increase when

A. All vehicles are moving at approximately the same speed
B. One lane of traffic is significantly slower than the rest
C. Where there is a traffic jam
D. A single vehicle is either exceeding or falling behind the traffic's pace

Q134/ When a sign or signal instructs you to stop, where should you stop your vehicle?

A. 15 feet after passing stop lines and crosswalk lines
B. You don't need to stop if there is no marked stop line
C. Behind stop lines and crosswalk lines
D. At whatever distance you perceive as a safe stopping distance

Q135/ When exiting a highway, what is the recommended distance for signaling to others with your turn signal?

A. At least 100 feet before the exit.
B. At least 250 feet before the exit.
C. At least 500 feet before the exit.
D. At least 1,000 feet before the exit

Q136/ When is it permissible to pass on the shoulder?

A. It is strictly not allowed
B. Only when you have a paved shoulder on the right side, and a vehicle is moving towards the left
C. Only when you have an unpaved shoulder on the right side, and a vehicle is moving toward the left
D. When a vehicle in front of you is moving at a very slow pace

Q137/ In North Carolina, what is the rule regarding making a right turn on a red light?

A. You are required to wait for a green light before turning right
B. You are allowed to make a right turn on red without stopping
C. You can make a right turn on red after a complete stop unless otherwise posted
D. You should only make a right turn on red during rush hour

Q138/ What are the most important guidelines and regulations about driving in construction areas

A. Reduce your speed even if there is no sign indicating this action
B. Paying extra attention to road signs, flashing lights or any traffic control system
C. Merge with caution and maintain a safe following time
D. A, B & C are all correct, hence D is the right answer

Q139/How close to a fire hydrant may you legally park?

A. Around 50 feet
B. Around 10 feet
C. Around 15 in either direction
D. Around 20 to 25 feet

Q140/ What are the factors that can negatively affect your braking distance?

A. Weather and road conditions, such as slippery roads due to snow or rain.
B. Your speed.
C. The condition of your tires, brakes, and braking oil.
D. A, B & C are all correct, hence D is the right answer

Q141/ What are the correct measures to follow if another driver indicates that they intend to overtake and pass your car?

A. Wait until the overtaking car has fully passed while maintaining your current speed.
B. Move to the left to obstruct the passing car.
C. Encourage the other driver to accelerate.
D. Politely inform the other motorist to maintain a safe distance behind you and not attempt to pass.

Q142/ Is the driver responsible for ensuring seat belt usage by their passengers?

A. Only when all passengers are above the age of 18
B. When passengers are at least sixteen years old
C. Yes, the driver is responsible for ensuring that all passengers wear seatbelts, and that each passenger under age 16 is properly secured in a child passenger restraint system
D. When passengers are under sixteen years old, they are exempt from this responsibility

Q143/ Choose from the following the most crucial moment to check traffic behind you

A. Backing, making an illegal U-turn, or at junction
B. In case you are entering a highway, freeway or a general road
C. Backing, crossing a railway crossing, or a drawbridge
D. Backing up, merging lanes, or slowing down

Q144/ If another vehicle creates a hazard by suddenly cutting in front of you. Which of these actions should you take first?

A. Take your foot off the gas
B. Sound your horn and step on the brake firmly
C. Swerve into the lane next to you
D. Drive onto the shoulder

Q145/ In which of the following situations is making a U-turn both unsafe and illegal?

A. When the driver's vision is obstructed by a bridge, ramp, or tunnel within 500 feet.
B. On a bend or slope with a clear view in either direction of fewer than 500 feet.
C. In the proximity of a railway crossing or within 100 feet of a railway crossing.
D. In all of the above situations.

Q146/ In the state of North Carolina, if you have a Limited Learner Permit, what are the authorized driving hours during the first six months, while accompanied by your supervising driver?

A. Between 10 a.m. and 2 p.m.
B. From 5 a.m. to 9 p.m.
C. Only after 9 p.m.
D. Anytime during the day or night.

Q147/ At an intersection, what does a steady yellow traffic light signify?

A. Maintain your current speed
B. Increase your speed to clear the intersection before the light turns red
C. Be ready to stop for an impending red light
D. Reduce your speed and proceed carefully

Q148/ Which type of accidents is the most frequently observed on interstates?

A. Head-on collisions
B. Commercial vehicle accidents
C. Side collisions
D. Rear-end collisions

Q149/When you're preparing to make a right turn at an intersection, and there is a bicycle to your right, who has the right-of-way once the traffic light switches to green?"

A. The first one to move
B. The right of way is yours
C. Yield to the bicycle
D. It's up to courtesy

Q150/ In wintry or icy driving conditions, which actions are recommended?

A. Utilizing your cruise control is a safe practice
B. Modify your speed and turns with extra caution, compared to normal conditions
C. You should drive just as you would in regular weather
D. Accelerate your speed for better control

ANSWERS

PART 2 ANSWERS :

Q01/ The answer is C. It is riskier to drive at the maximum speed limit at night than it is during the day due **to reduced visibility**.

Q2/ The answer is D. You are legally intoxicated in North Carolina if your blood alcohol level **(BAC) is 0.08%** or above.

Q03/ The answer is B. For better traffic management and to avoid congestion **use the rightmost lane** to avoid interrupting the traffic flow.

Q04/ The answer is D. Traffic already at the roundabout has the right of way over traffic that is trying to enter.

Q05/ The answer is D. All of the aforementioned hand-held devices cause a prolonged perception time and increase the risk of accidents.

Q06/ The answer is C. The difference between the two is that controlled intersections are managed **via traffic control devices** such as signs and signals. Uncontrolled intersections, on the other hand, **rely on right-of-way rules and driver competency for traffic management**. They are also often found in rural areas

Q07/ The answer is D. Avoid slowing down to look at accidents on the roadways, as **it interferes with the smooth flow of traffic**

Q08/ The answer is D. A, B and C are all correct, hence D is the answer.

Q09/ The answer is D. The usage of guide dogs and white canes marks the presence of a blind pedestrian. This situation requires extra prudency and alertness from drivers, **especially the ones driving an electric or hybrid vehicle** as blind pedestrians rely on sound to identify their presence.

Q10/ The answer is C. No Parking is allowed in this area

Q11/ The answer is C. You are permitted to make a left turn at a red light. However, this is only allowed when you're on **a one-way street intending to enter another one-way street** with no prohibiting signage. Always exercise caution and yield to pedestrians while proceeding.

Q12/ The answer is C. Yellow solid lines convey two major pieces of information to road users, Firstly, they indicate that the line **separates traffic traveling in opposite directions**. Secondly, the fact that the line is solid, regardless of its color, signifies that **passing or turning is strictly prohibited.**

Q13/ The answer is C. It is vital to quickly glance over your shoulder while changing lanes **to identify vehicles in your blind spot** regardless of how you adjust your mirrors

Q14/ The answer is D. A shared center lane is distinguishable via double yellow lines, one set of broken yellow lines on the inside, and solid yellow lines on the outside. And is designated **for executing left turns or U-turns where permitted**

87

Q15/ The answer is C. **You have 60 days** to inform the DMV about the change of your address or update your name

Q16/ The answer is C. You are required by law to follow the instructions **of a flagger at a construction zone** to avoid hazards and congestion during unusual road conditions.

Q17/ The answer is B. **Gradually and safely come to a full stop** by moving to the **right side** of the road

Q18/The answer is D. The primary guideline for executing a safe and lawful turn involves positioning your vehicle in the appropriate lane **well in advance** of the turn. In the case of a left turn, it is customary to position your vehicle in **the leftmost lane,** unless there are signs, signals, or road markings specifying an alternative route

Q19/ The answer is A. **Never stop, back up, or try to turn in** an interstate highway as it will create a dangerous driving situation

Q20/ The answer is A. Even if the traffic lights turned green the pedestrian still has the right of way and he should complete his crossing. Always remember that driving requires courtesy and discipline.

Q21/The answer is C. If your driver's license is suspended due to the point system in North Carolina, it may be taken away for the first suspension **for 60 Days**

Q22/ The answer is D. Avoid **obstructing an intersection**, even when an emergency vehicle is on its way. If you're in an intersection and you hear or see an emergency vehicle

approaching, proceed through the intersection first. henceforth, pull over to the right at the earliest safe opportunity and come to a stop.

Q23/ The answer is A. Different types of drinks have no different effects on you. It is **the amount of alcohol** you consume that elevates your blood alcohol concentration.

Q24/ The answer is C. You are required by law to **notify the police** about the incident.

Q25/ The answer is B. As a wise driver, you are responsible for making roadways safe, This is why the best decision to make where traffic flow is congested on intersections is to remain calm, **not proceed until the junction is cleared**, and then you can go. Making a U-turn can be unsafe in such circumstances and sounding your horns can lead to an aggressive reaction from irresponsible road users.

Q26/ The answer is B. In conditions of reduced visibility use your **low-beam headlights** for better vision.

Q27/ The answer is C. According to the right-of-way hierarchy, vehicles that are already at the intersection should be given the way and then vehicles on the right.

Q28/ The answer is D. All of the answers are correct about skidding, to avoid this situation always **drive at a lower speed** when weather conditions are adverse.

Q29/ The answer is A. Law enforcement officers, such as police or peace officers, should be obeyed over traffic control signals and signs for better traffic management and safety. They have the authority to direct traffic and override the usual rules when necessary.

Q30/ The answer is D. The minimum liability insurance required for covering all personal injuries in a crash **is $60,000**.

Q31/ The answer is D. You must dim your headlights to low beams whenever you are **within 500 feet of an approaching vehicle** or **within 300 feet of a vehicle you are following**.

Q32/ The answer is C. Hydroplaning happens when your tires lose their grip due to **weather-related** causes and leads to a **degradation of steering** and braking control

Q33/ The answer is D. Ease off the accelerator and downshift to a lower gear. This action will create a braking effect, slowing down the vehicle, a technique known as **engine braking**

Q34/ The answer B. The statement is true. However, there are countries where traffic travels in a **clockwise direction** at roundabouts. Such as Japan and the United Kingdom

Q35/ The answer B. Increase your following distance to avoid the risk of a collision on the roadways

Q36/ The answer is B. Driving with a suspended license **is not allowed** under any circumstance and convictions for such an offense lead to the exacerbation of the penalty

Q37/ The answer is B. Always **Decelerate** before entering a curve

Q38/ The answer is D. Uneven distribution of weight around the tire can lead to the pulling of the vehicle on one side of the road, vibration, and increased fuel consumption

Q39/ The answer is A. Make sure that you have good visibility, use your turn signal, and that there is no sign that prohibits passing

Q40/ The answer is A. Always begin and end a left turn **in the far left lane in the direction you are traveling**, unless signs or surface markings indicate otherwise. To make a turn far in advance and merge into the far left lane when the path is clear

Q41/ The answer is D. Look at the **right side** of the road and avoid a direct look at the lights

Q42/ The answer is D. All of the answers mentioned above cause a prolonged reaction time

Q43/ The answer is C. It is not considered safe to pass and overtake and is strictly not allowed.

Q44/ The answer is D. A **temporary alternative roadway** to avoid congestion or bypass a closed road

Q45/ The answer is C. Treat the intersection **as a yield sign**, meaning you should slow down and stop if necessary and give the right-of-way

Q46/ The answer is C. According to North Carolina insurance law, the minimum requirement **for bodily injury liability** coverage to any person per accident is **$30,000.**

Q47/ The answer is C. You are required to give the right of way to vehicles coming from the opposite direction

Q48/ The answer is A. When the **road is wet**, it's advisable to reduce your speed to maintain better control of your vehicle and ensure safety. Driving 5 to 10 MPH under the posted speed limit is a recommended practice in wet conditions.

Q49/ The answer is D. Treat this situation as if it were a **four-way stop sign**, meaning that you should stop and yield to the vehicle

Q50/ The answer is A. Highway hypnosis is a condition characterized by drowsiness due to the monotony of long drives. To counteract it, it's advisable to regularly **shift your gaze and focus on different objects.**

Q51/ The answer is C. The seatbelt system should be used for children under 8 years old and weighing less than 80 pounds is a weight-appropriate child passenger restraint system

Q52/ The answer is D. Your driver's license **is personal** and can't be shared under any circumstances.

Q53/ The answer is B. The vehicle **on the right has** the right of way under these circumstances. To add, pedestrians and other vulnerable road users have the same driving privileges.

Q54/ The answer is B. Call the local authorities and ask for an ambulance

Q55/ The answer is A. They tend to freeze before the rest of the road does.

Q56/ The answer is B. The **two-second** rule refers to the minimum guideline for the following time.

Q57/ The answer is C. Yield the right of way **to traffic already on the highway** if you can't safely mesh into traffic even if there is no posted sign indicating this instruction

Q58/ The answer is C. Ensuring the safety of children is a critical concern while driving. Exercise heightened caution in school zones and refrain from overtaking other vehicles. Stay attentive!

Q59/ The answer is C. because **oil on the road surface** can make construction zones **slippery**, especially when wet and when oil and water are mixed. The other answers can influence your perception and reaction time. Therefore, if the question was about the **STOPPING time/distance** (the sum of perception/reaction/braking time/distance), the answer would've been all the aforementioned options

Q60/The answer is B. They must have **a licensed person** accompany them and sit beside them in the vehicle.

Q61/The answer is B. Large trucks have **wider blind spots**. Thus, you need to drive with extra caution alongside commercial vehicles

Q62/ The answer is A. The correct hand signal to indicate a left turn while driving is to **extend your hand and arm outward** from the driver's side window

Q63/ The answer is B. Only allowed if you have a **disabled parking permit**

Q64/ The answer is D. All of the options on this quiz provide great instructions to reduce the possibility of hydroplaning **90**

Q65/ The answer is C. Point your wheels away from the curb and then roll back slowly so that the rear part of the right front wheel rests against the curb. The curb **will block your car from rolling backward** if your brakes fail.

Q66/ The answer is A. Treat the intersection as if it was controlled **via a stop sign**.

Q67/ The answer is C. If you're a recent arrival and have just established residency, you **have a 60-day** window to acquire a North Carolina driver's license or learner permit.

Q68/ The answer is B. High-beam headlights should be used when driving on **unlit rural roads** because they provide maximum illumination and help you see further ahead. In such conditions, there are typically no streetlights and high beams can improve visibility without causing glare for other drivers.

Q69/ The answer is C. All of the mentioned measures in options A & and B manage sun glare.

Q70/ The answer is C. This combination of signals indicates that you are only allowed to proceed in **the direction indicated** by the green **arrow** without stopping.

Q71/ The answer is D. This correctly highlights the various issues that can arise from unbalanced tires or low tire pressures.

Q72/ The answer is C. Performing a shoulder check helps ensure you're aware of any vehicles or hazards in your **blind spots,** enhancing safety while driving.

Q73/ The answer is C. Immature and aggressive maneuvers that **endanger road** users and lead to collisions and is considered an infraction of traffic laws

Q74/ The answer is D. All of these statements are correct because they can create hazards on the road and the likelihood of collisions

Q75/ The answer is B. If your chemical test indicates a **BAC of 0.08%** or higher, your driver's license will be suspended for a **minimum of 30 days**

Q76/ The answer is D. You will **block the visibility of** other road users and create more hazards on the road

Q77/ The answer is B. Motorcycles sometimes need to pull to the right or left side of their lane to avoid hazardous road conditions or to be noticed by other cars. A cautionary space is required

Q78/ The answer is C. The maximum speed limit on interstate highways typically is **70 mph** under ideal driving conditions

Q79/ The answer is B. Before attempting to pass another vehicle on a multilane highway, it's essential to **check your rearview mirror** to ensure there are no vehicles approaching from behind at a high speed.

Q79/ The answer is B. Before attempting to pass another vehicle on a multilane highway, it's essential to **check your rearview mirror** to ensure there are no vehicles approaching from behind at a high speed.

Q80/ The answer is C. When approaching a railroad crossing protected by flashing red lights, a motor vehicle must **come to a full stop,** maintaining a distance of not less than fifteen feet and not more **than fifty feet** from the nearest track

Q81/ The answer is B. Never move an injured body off the road as it can cause more damage instead protect the scene of the accident

Q82/ The answer is D. When there's not enough room for a U-turn, **a three-point** turn is a commonly used

Q83/ The answer is B. Changing lanes on a multi-lane roundabout **is prohibited** either explicitly in certain jurisdictions or implicitly as there is a high risk of a collision.

Q84/ The answer is A. You **should not pass** between them and wait until they allow you to pass.

Q85/ The answer is A. Child safety is a very important issue when driving, always be extra cautious in school zone areas, never pass another vehicle, pay attention to school buses when their lights are flashing, and obey the posted or statutory speed limits

Q86/ The answer is C. When you're at the crest of a grade where your vehicle cannot be seen by traffic from the opposite direction, **making a U-turn is unsafe** as it can lead to collisions with vehicles you cannot see coming over the crest of the hill

Q87/ The answer is A. Always **pull over and park** before answering the call unless you are answering from a hands-free device

Q88/ The answer is D. When your BAC **reaches 0.05% or higher**, your risk of a traffic accident rises. At this level, you may experience reduced coordination, and diminished ability to track moving objects.

Q89/ The answer is B. If your license is revoked due to your refusal to undergo chemical testing you could potentially qualify for restricted driving privileges **after 6 months of the revocation** period have passed.

Q90/ The answer is D. Tapping your horn **isn't a** necessary measure and sometimes can be a misplaced gesture

Q91/ The answer is C. Maintain firm pressure on the brake while steering to use ABS brakes

Q92/ The answer is C. The heavier the vehicle and the faster it is moving, the **longer it takes to safely stop**

Q93/ The answer is A. Carbon monoxide can accumulate inside your vehicle when the windows are closed or in your garage if your engine is idling. Initial signs of carbon monoxide poisoning encompass **sudden fatigue, headaches, dizziness, and nausea.** In case you encounter these symptoms, it's crucial to act by opening the windows, turning off the ignition, or exiting the vehicle or garage for your safety

Q94/ The answer is A. White lane marking separate traffic **traveling in the same direction**

Q95/ The answer is C. In cities and towns, the default speed limit unless otherwise posted **is 35 mph**

Q96/ The answer is B. A lane marked with a diamond symbol is **a HOV only** lane and/or it is reserved for taxis/buses/bicycles

Q97/ The answer is B. Between **half an hour of sunset and half an hour of sunrise,** and at any other time when **visibility is low**

Q98/ The answer is A. If you reach a junction as the traffic signals turn red, you should **exit the intersection** as safely as possible and avoid blocking it.

Q99/ The answer is D. If you hold a Limited Learner Permit, no one except the driver and the supervising driver are allowed to be in the front seat

Q100/ The answer is A. It is crucial to be vigilant and look carefully for motorcycles when changing lanes **because their smaller size can make them less visible** to other drivers

Q101/ The answer is C. Cautiously move to **the non-designated parking** space on the rightmost part of the road, close to the edge, and turn on your emergency flashers to alert oncoming traffic

Q102/ The answer is B. According to North Carolina insurance law, the minimum amount of liability insurance required for property damage in a crash **is $25,000.**

Q103/ The answer is C. Passing on the right is legal in specific situations. The driver of a vehicle may pass on the right if the roadway is **free from obstruction** and of sufficient width for two or more lines of moving vehicles, and when the vehicle being overtaken is either making or about **to make a left turn or is on a one-way street**

Q104/ The answer is A. The vehicle traveling downhill must **yield the right-of-way by backing up** until the vehicle going uphill can pass

Q105/ The answer is C. Smoking or eating marijuana **impairs a driver's ability to respond to sights and sounds,** making them less capable of handling quick tasks and significantly decreasing their responsiveness, especially when facing unexpected events on the road.

Q106/ The answer is D. All of the mentioned answers in options A,B and C represent situations where passing is strictly prohibited

Q107/ The answer is B. The primary cause of rear-end crashes on highways is **following too closely**, commonly referred to as "tailgating."

Q108/ The answer is C. In areas with playing children, while driving you should expect Potential sudden, inattentive running in front of your vehicle

Q109/ The answer is B. In the event of a sudden flat tire while driving, firmly grip the steering wheel to maintain a straight course. **Gradually reduce your speed** by removing your foot from the accelerator and gently apply the brakes

Q110/The answer is C. A red arrow signal at an intersection indicates that **you are not allowed to turn in the direction of the arrow**.

Q111/ The answer is A. While it's crucial to exchange, determining fault is **a matter for insurance companies** and authorities to decide based on the available evidence.

Q112/ The answer is C. The minimum duration of license revocation if you are convicted of driving more than 15 miles per hour over the speed limit, and your speed exceeds 55 mph **is 30 days**

Q113/ The answer is D. On a two-lane, two-way road, **a broken yellow** line indicates that you are allowed to cross over into the opposing lane

Q114/The answer is A. In a situation where your vehicle has stalled on railroad tracks and a train is approaching, your top priority is **the safety of yourself and your passengers.** You should immediately exit the vehicle and move as far away from the tracks as possible to ensure your safety

Q115/The answer is C. Before opening the door of your parked vehicle on a roadside, it's essential to **check and ensure** that doing so will not pose a danger to anyone

Q116/ The answer is C. Yield to vehicles as you are merging to make your maneuver safer.

Q117/ The answer is C. Flaggers are present at construction sites to **optimize traffic flow** and help drivers avoid hazards. you are required to follow their instructions

Q118/ The answer is D. If your license is revoked because you declined to undergo chemical testing, the DMV will extend your suspension for a minimum **of 12 months**.

Q119/ The answer is C. In North Carolina, you must report any motor vehicle crash **that causes $1,000** or more in property damage or if the accident caused **injury or death**

Q120/ The answer is D. Orange signs, flaggers, and pylons

Q121/ The answer is A. Never cross the railroad track unless there is room on the other side.

Q122/ The answer is C. All drivers are required to carry Liability insurance coverage

Q123/ The answer is C. When you apply **intense braking force** at high speeds, the brakes' strength can surpass the road's traction capacity. This can lead to the wheels locking up, resulting in the vehicle skidding.

Q124/ The answer is C. If you're below the age of 21, NC has a zero tolerance law **0.00%**

Q125/ The answer C. Turn the steering **wheel in the direction** you intend for the front wheels to move. If your rear wheels begin sliding in the opposite direction as you regain control, gently adjust the steering wheel to that side

Q126/ The answer is B. You have the right of way as both vehicles arrived at **the same time** and you are **on the right**

Q127/ The answer is C. For better traffic management **use the leftmost lane,** however, do not tailgate, drive aggressively, or pass irresponsibly slower vehicles on this lane.

94

Q128/ The answer is D. Hands-free devices feature all of the options.

Q129/ The answer is C. the recommended seatbelt usage for all occupants in a vehicle is Both lap and shoulder belts on every trip

Q130/ The answer is C. The addition of the perception, reaction, and braking distance.

Q131/ The answer is D. Edge forward cautiously, check for both traffic and pedestrians, and proceed once it's safe

Q132/ The answer is B. when it may help **prevent a collision**

Q133/ The answer is D. collisions tend to decrease if all the vehicle maintains the same speed

Q134/ The answer is C. When a sign or signal requires you to stop, you should come to a **complete stop** behind the designated stop lines and crosswalk lines

Q135/ The answer is C. It's advisable to signal your intentions by using your signal at **least 500 feet** before the exit

Q136/ The answer is B. Only when you have a paved shoulder on the right, and a vehicle is moving to **the left**

Q137/ The answer is C. You can turn right on red unless a posted sign is prohibiting the maneuver.

Q138/ The answer is D. All of these instructions are correct

Q139/ The answer is C. Stay at least **15 feet away** from a fire hydrant in either direction

Q140/ The answer is D. The speed of traveling, the condition of your vehicle tires, the weather play a major role in extending **the braking time**

Q141/ The answer is A. Wait until the overtaking car has fully passed while maintaining your present speed

Q142/ The answer is C. Yes, the driver is responsible for ensuring that **all passengers wear seatbelts**, and children should be properly secured in a **child restraint system**

Q143/The answer is D. Using shoulder checks is an effective way to check your blind spots prior to **backing up/ merging lanes/slowing down**

Q144/ The answer is C. Swerve into the lane next to you

Q145/ The answer is D. All the answers indicate situations where making a U-turn is prohibited due to a high risk of collision.

Q146/ The answer is B. In the state of North Carolina, If you have a Limited Learner Permit, the authorized driving hours during the first six months, while accompanied by your supervising driver is **from 5 a.m. to 9 p.m.**

Q147/ The answer is C. Be prepared to stop and **gradually** lower your speed prior to stopping

Q148/ The answer is D. Rear-end collisions are the most frequent crashes on interstates

Q149/ The answer is C. The bicycle has the right of way

Q150/ The answer is B. Reduce your speed and turns with extra caution

Made in the USA
Columbia, SC
20 July 2024

39073059R00052